A GUIDE TO BIRD CLASSIFICATION

FAMILIES
OF BIRDS

by
OLIVER L. AUSTIN, JR.
Illustrated by
ARTHUR SINGER

Original Project Editor
HERBERT S. ZIM

GOLDEN PRESS • NEW YORK
Western Publishing Company, Inc.
Racine, Wisconsin

FOREWORD

This guide to the framework of bird classification presents thumbnail sketches of the 34 orders (29 living, 5 fossil) and 185 families (150 living, 35 fossil) into which scientists currently group the some 9,600 known species (8,700 living, 900 fossil) of birds in the world. It is designed for those who have familiarity with birds and would like to know more about their relationships to one another. This guide differs from its predecessors in the Golden Field Guide series in that it emphasizes groups of animals instead of the basic unit, the species. The illustrations in this guide are of species selected on the basis of typical family characteristics.

This edition has been completely revised and updated to conform to the sequences and nomenclature of the A.O.U. *Check-list of North American Birds*, 6th Edition, 1983.

O.L.A., Jr.

CONTENTS

INTRODUCTION

The class of vertebrates known as AVES comprises one of the most distinctive and, to judge by the steadily increasing interest being shown in them, most delightful and pleasing of the animals that share the earth with man.

Scientists subdivide the class Aves for convenience into categories, or "taxa," designed to express relationships. Each taxon is, theoretically at least, a monophyletic group, its members stemming from a single common ancestor. The basic taxon is the *species*–essentially a group of individuals capable of reproducing themselves by interbreeding. Closely related species are gathered into the next higher taxon, the *genus*, and the double-barreled scientific name of each animal and plant is made up of its generic and specific names.

Related genera are gathered into *families*, and families in turn into *orders*. It is often necessary (and convenient) to recognize intermediate groups—subclasses, superorders, suborders, superfamilies, subfamilies, and tribes. American ornithologists have standardized the endings of the names of the higher taxa—all orders end in "iformes," all families end in "idae," subfamilies in "inae," and tribes in "inie" (page 10).

Scientific names and common names (where they exist) are both given in this guide. While scientific names may have little meaning to the nonprofessional, they are the very foundation of taxonomy.

The criteria for defining the orders and families, as well as other taxa, are mainly anatomical, but habits, behavior, and geographical distribution are also of significance, and are outlined here for each taxon. The inclusive lengths given in inches under "Characteristics" and for the species illustrated are the standard measurement of the bird from tip of bill to tip of tail. They are the most convenient indication of comparative sizes available.

FAUNAL REGIONS OF THE WORLD

Geographical distribution and classification go hand in hand. Despite the great mobility their powers of flight give birds, most species, families, and orders are limited to definite, restricted ranges. The ranges of practically no two species or groups are exactly alike, except for those limited to certain small islands, yet those of many are somewhat similar, suggesting basic relationships.

Zoologists divide the world into faunal regions. The faunas of each region are comparatively uniform and self-contained. The names of these regions are a great convenience in referring to these large areas of natural zoological significance. The ranges given for each family are as comprehensive and detailed as space limitations permit.

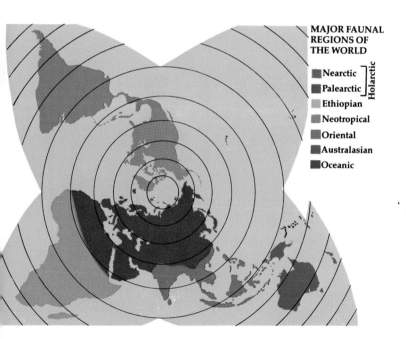

MAJOR FAUNAL
REGIONS OF
THE WORLD

Nearctic ⎤
Palearctic ⎦ Holarctic
Ethiopian
Neotropical
Oriental
Australasian
Oceanic

THE FOSSIL RECORD provides most of our knowledge of the evolutionary development of birds. The record for birds is relatively scant, but it is now enough to give us some idea of the composition of bird faunas of past geological ages. The accompanying graph shows the percentages of each order of birds known from each of the

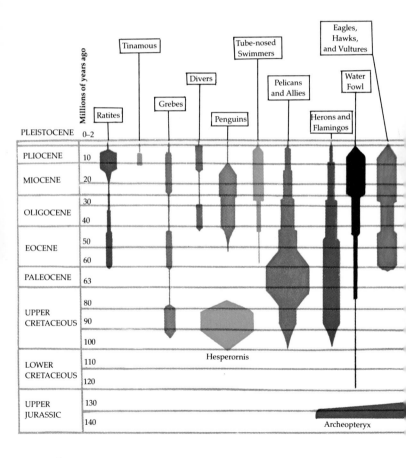

major epochs and periods. The figures are biased in favor of the water birds and the larger flightless ground birds because of their greater likelihood of being fossilized. Despite this bias, the graph shows a steady decline of the more primitive non-passerine orders and a steady increase in the perching birds.

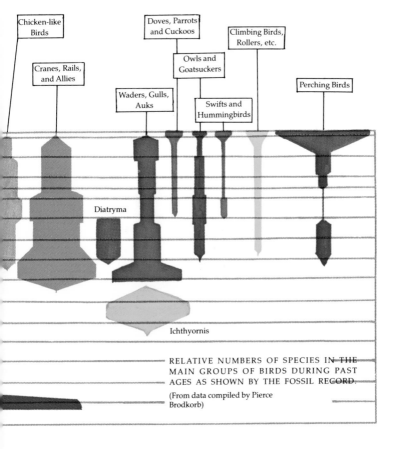

RELATIVE NUMBERS OF SPECIES IN THE MAIN GROUPS OF BIRDS DURING PAST AGES AS SHOWN BY THE FOSSIL RECORD.

(From data compiled by Pierce Brodkorb)

ORIGIN AND EVOLUTION OF BIRDS

Birds are believed to have arisen in early Mesozoic time, more than 150 million years ago, from reptilian ancestors—probably running or tree-climbing dinosaurs. The earliest fossil bird known, Archaeopteryx (page 12) of the Upper Jurassic was reptilian in structure, and only its clearly delineated feathers distinguish it from some of the small dinosaurs of the same period.

The fossil record of birds is still rather fragmentary. Nevertheless, some 1,750 bird species have been identified from fossil remains. About 850 of these are species

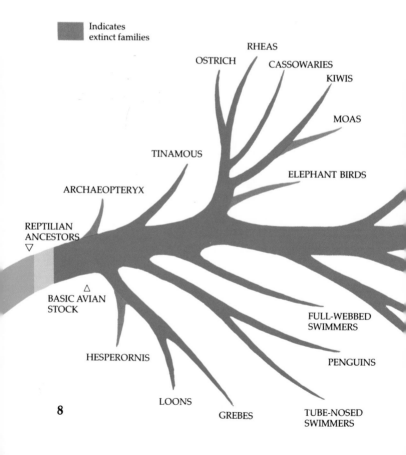

Indicates
extinct families

RHEAS
OSTRICH
CASSOWARIES
KIWIS
MOAS
TINAMOUS
ELEPHANT BIRDS
ARCHAEOPTERYX
REPTILIAN
ANCESTORS
▽
△
BASIC AVIAN
STOCK
FULL-WEBBED
SWIMMERS
HESPERORNIS
PENGUINS
LOONS
GREBES
TUBE-NOSED
SWIMMERS

still living today but whose ancestry goes back some 2 million years to late Pliocene time. The other 900 species are known only as fossils. Each fossil taxon is indicated by a standard printer's dagger sign (†) preceding its name.

The tree on these pages shows the probable development of the main orders of birds. Most of these are believed to have arisen before or during Eocene time, 50 million years ago. The orders and families of birds are arranged in this guide to follow the evolutionary development from the most primitive to the modern.

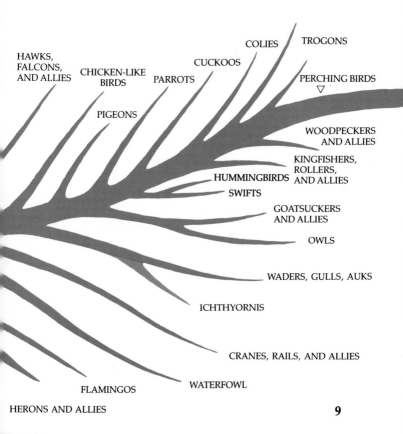

AMERICAN ROBIN, *Turdus migratorius*

TABLE OF ORGANIZATION

KINGDOM:	Animalia (animals as opposed to plants)
PHYLUM:	Chordata (notochord)
SUBPHYLUM:	Vertebrata (a backbone of vertebrae)
CLASS:	Aves (the birds)
SUBCLASS:	Neornithes (true birds with no teeth)
SUPERORDER:	Neognathae (keeled birds)
ORDER:	Passeriformes (perching birds)
FAMILY:	Muscicapidae (Old World Flycatchers)
SUBFAMILY:	Turdinae (thrushes)
GENUS:	*Turdus*
SPECIES:	*migratorius*

BIRDS
CLASS AVES

Birds are warm-blooded vertebrates with a four-chambered heart. They have scales on their legs and feet, and are distinguished from all other animals by the possession of feathers. To state it simply, if a creature has feathers, it is a bird; if it hasn't, it isn't.

The skeleton of a bird is modified for flight: bones are lightened; vertebrae, pelvic and shoulder girdles are fused into a strong, light body case; and a keeled sternum anchors muscles to give power to a bird's wings. Those lacking a keel on their breastbone are the relatively few flightless running birds. It is the birds' mastery of flight that gives them their strongest attraction for man.

TOPOGRAPHY OF A BIRD

crown
forehead
lores
upper mandible
lower mandible
eye ring
chin
throat
whisker
breast
side
belly
flanks
median line
eye stripe
eye line
nape
ear patch
back

LARK SPARROW
Chondestes grammacus

shoulder
wing bars
rump
upper tail coverts
tail
secondaries
tarsus
primaries
outer tail feathers

SUBCLASS SAURIURAE—
Toothed Reptile–like Birds

† ARCHAEOPTERYX—Archaeopterygiformes

Contains a single fossil family of land birds (known from remains well preserved in European limestone).

† ARCHAEOPTERYX, Archaeopterygidae

Distribution: 2 species, Bavarian Upper Jurassic deposits about 130,000,000 years old. Four specimens known.

Characteristics: 20″ Jaws with teeth set in sockets. Clavicles fused into wishbone, but sternum unkeeled. Claws on bend of wing; pelvic bones unfused; separate tail vertebrae, each supporting pair of feathers. Reptile-like in many characters, but had feathers, hence earliest true birds known. Probably capable of weak soaring, perhaps flapping, flight.

ARCHAEOPTERYX

SUBCLASS ODONTOHOLCAE—
Toothed Diving Birds

†HESPERORNIS—Hesperornithiformes

Contains a single fossil family of North American water birds.

†HESPERORNIS, Hesperornithidae

Distribution: 4 species, Kansas and Montana, in Upper Cretaceous deposits about 90,000,000 years old. Fossils of this family are fairly plentiful.

Characteristics: 54″. Jaws with teeth in furrows. Wing bones greatly reduced, sternum unkeeled. Pelvic bones unfused, but tail vertebrae fused into a pygostyle. Large flightless swimming and diving birds, somewhat resembling loons. Most remains found with marine fossils of the Cretaceous seas.

HESPERORNIS

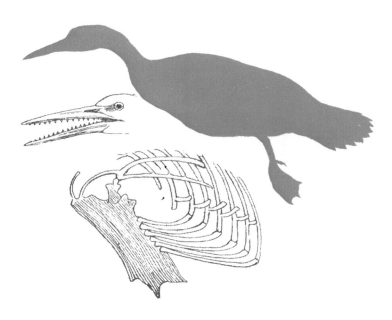

SUPERORDER PALEOGNATHAE—Tinamous.
Primitive running ground birds, probably nearest to the ancestral stock from which all living birds descended.

TINAMOUS—Tinamiformes

Contains a single family of South American ground birds.

TINAMOUS, Tinamidae

Distribution: 44 species, 40 living, 14 fossil, earliest Pliocene of Argentina. Mexico to Patagonia; in heavy jungles, scrub and grass lands, alpine slopes. Nonmigratory.

Characteristics: 8–22″. Sternum keeled, wings and tail short, toes 3 or 4. Distinctive ratite-like palate. Sexes similar, females often slightly larger. Plumage brownish, barred, streaked, or mottled.

Habits: Run rapidly, fly strongly for short distances. Eat seeds, fruit, berries, some insects. Eggs 1–10, brightly colored, highly glossed. Male incubates in ground nest and rears highly precocial young.

TAWNY-BREASTED TINAMOU 15″
Nothocercus julius
Venezuela, Colombia, Ecuador

THICKET TINAMOU 11″
Crypturellus cinnamomeus
Mexico to Costa Rica,
Colombia, Venezuela

sternum
(keeled)

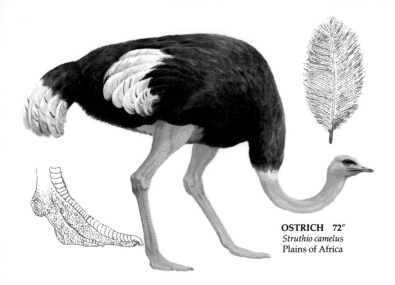

OSTRICH 72″
Struthio camelus
Plains of Africa

SUPERORDER RATITAE—Ratite Birds. Two fossil and six living orders of flightless running birds, distinguished by unkeeled sternum.

OSTRICHES—Struthioniformes

Contains 1 fossil and 1 living family of large Old World ratites.

†ELEUTHERORNIS, Eleutherornithidae
The single fossil species is known by a fragmentary pelvis from the Eocene of Switzerland.

OSTRICHES, Struthionidae
Distribution: 8 species, 1 living, 8 fossil, earliest Pliocene of Eurasia. Living species now restricted to Africa (formerly Asia Minor) in deserts, dry plains. Nonmigratory.
Characteristics: 72″ (height 8′). Largest living birds. Toes 2, thighs bare, wing and tail plumes ornamental only. Male, black and white; female, gray and white; chick, dappled.
Habits: Travel in small flocks, often with herds of ungulates. Eat seeds, berries, plants, small animals. Polygamous, two or more hens lay 2 to 10 eggs each in same nest. Male incubates mostly at night, hens by day.

RHEAS—Rheiformes

Contains 1 fossil and 1 living family of large South American ratites.

†OPISTHODACTYLUS, Opisthodactylidae

The single fossil species is known by a leg bone from the Lower Eocene of southern Patagonia.

RHEAS, Rheidae

Distribution: 5 species, 2 living, 4 fossil, earliest *Heterorhea* of Upper Pliocene of northern Argentina. 2 living species found in Brazil and Peru to Patagonia, in dry plains and open foothills. Nonmigratory.

Characteristics: 32–52" (height 5'). Heaviest of New World birds. Toes 3, thighs feathered, wings very short, tail plumes lacking. Plumage is soft, filmy, grayish in color.

Habits: Travel in flocks, often with large mammals. Food largely vegetable, some insects, small animals. Polygamous; several hens deposit 20 to 50 eggs in same nest, which male incubates.

COMMON RHEA   52"
Rhea americana
Brazil, Uruguay, Argentina

sternum
(unkeeled)

AUSTRALIAN CASSOWARY 65"
Casuarius casuarius
Northern Australia, New Guinea

CASSOWARIES AND EMUS—Casuariiformes

One fossil and 2 living families of large, flightless runners with stout legs, strong feet, 3 toes; plumage coarse, heavy, drooping; no tail quills. Australo-Papuan region.

CASSOWARIES, Casuariidae

Distribution: 4 species, 3 living, 1 fossil in Upper Pleistocene of Australia. Living forms in New Guinea, adjacent islands, and n. Australia; in heavy forest. Nonmigratory.

Characteristics: 52–68" (height 5'). Bony casque on naked varicolored head; 3–6 wirelike wing quills; spikelike nail on inner toe. Plumage largely black; female larger than male.

Habits: Live alone, or in pairs, or small flocks. Swim well; bad-tempered. Eat fruit, berries, plants, insects, small animals. Eggs 3–6, incubated by male; both sexes rear young.

EMUS, Dromaiidae

Distribution: 6 species, 1 living, 3 recently extinct, 5 fossil in Upper Pleistocene of Australia. Living form in Australia in open plains and semideserts. Nonmigratory.

Characteristics: 78″ (height 6′). Head and neck are partly feathered, no casque, wings are rudimentary. Sexes are similar, grayish brown above, lighter below; male is larger than female; chicks are striped.

Habits: Travel in flocks. Swim well; not bad-tempered. Eat fruit, berries, some insects, fond of caterpillars. Eggs 7–10, incubated by male; both parents rear young.

† DROMORNIS, Dromornithidae

Two fossil species from Upper Pleistocene of Australia. *Dromornis* has been identified by its leg bones alone, *Genyornis* by the restoration of an entire skeleton.

EMU   78″
Dromiceius novaehollandiae
Plains of Australia

†MOAS—Dinornithiformes

Two fossil families from the Pliocene and Quaternary of New Zealand.

†LESSER MOAS, Emeidae

Distribution: 19 fossil and subfossil species, earliest Lower Pliocene, latest perhaps mid-19th century.

Characteristics: Height 3–7′. Wings rudimentary or absent. Legs stout, toes 4. Coarse feathers with long aftershaft.

Habits: Probably grazers and browsers; fed on leaves, grass, fruit, seeds.

†GREAT MOAS, Dinornithidae

Distribution: 8 fossil species from Quaternary.

Characteristics: Height 6–10′. Largest weighed perhaps 500 pounds. Similar to Lesser Moas in general characteristics and habits.

†ELEPHANT BIRDS—Aepyornithiformes

†ELEPHANT BIRDS, Aepyornithidae

Distribution: 9 fossil species, North Africa in Eocene and Oligocene strata, Madagascar in Quaternary deposits.

Characteristics: Height 3–9′. Massive body on short, heavy legs. Toes 3. The largest Madagascar species was the heaviest bird known, weighing about 1,000 pounds. Its tremendous egg held 2 gallons.

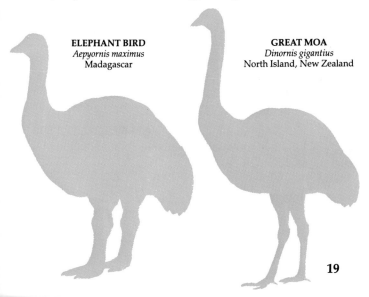

ELEPHANT BIRD
Aepyornis maximus
Madagascar

GREAT MOA
Dinornis gigantius
North Island, New Zealand

KIWIS—Apterygiformes

The smallest of the primitive flightless birds; are strangely unbirdlike.

KIWIS, Apterygidae

Distribution: 4 species, 3 living, 4 as fossils from New Zealand Quaternary sites. Living forms limited to wooded swamps in New Zealand.

Characteristics: 18–33″ (height 1′), weight 3 to 9 pounds. Wings rudimentary, tail absent, legs short and stout, toes 3. Nostrils open at tip of long, flexible bill. Feathers coarse, hairy, without aftershaft. Brown or grayish in color, sexes similar; female larger than male.

Habits: Solitary nocturnal birds. Probe in wet ground for worms, also eat insects, berries, plant shoots. Lay 1–2 huge eggs (they weigh about 1 pound) in underground burrow. Incubation by male.

BROWN KIWI 25″
Apteryx australis
South Island, New Zealand

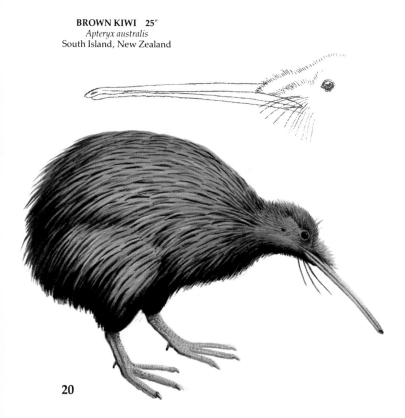

SUPERORDER NEOGNATHAE—Carinate Birds.

These are the flying birds, distinguished by having a keeled sternum. The superorder includes all the rest of the Class Aves.

LOONS—Gaviiformes

Contains 2 fossil families and 1 living family of swimming and diving birds.

†ENALIORNIS, Enaliornithidae

2 fossil species from the Lower Cretaceous of England, known only by a few leg bones.

†LONCHODYTES, Lonchodytidae

2 fossil species from the Upper Cretaceous of Wyoming, known only by a few leg and wing bones.

LOONS, Gaviidae

Distribution: 12 species, 4 living, 12 fossil, earliest Upper Paleocene, France. Living forms in northern parts of Northern Hemisphere; breed on fresh water; winter on salt water; migratory.

Characteristics: 24–40″. Legs at end of body. 3 front toes fully webbed. Wings narrow, pointed; tail short, stiff. Plumage heavy, waterproof, black and white or gray above, white below. Sexes alike.

Habits: Fairly strong fliers; expert swimmers and divers. Swim with feet. Eat fish, some insects, crustacea. Nest on ground close to water. Eggs 2, brown spotted with black. Both sexes incubate and rear young.

ARCTIC LOON   25″
Gavia arctica
Northern Eurasia; Alaska to Hudson Bay

GREBES—Podicipediformes

An order containing 1 fossil and 1 living family of swimming and diving birds.

†BAPTORNIS, Baptornithidae

2 fossil species known by leg bones of Upper Cretaceous age, *Baptornis* from Kansas, and *Neogaeornis* from Chile.

GREBES, Podicipedidae

Distribution: 29 species, 18 living, 20 fossil, earliest from Miocene of Oregon. Living forms in fresh waters the world around except oceania; a few winter on salt water. Some migratory.

Characteristics: 10–28". Legs at end of body, all 4 toes lobate-webbed. Wings short, curved; tail very short. Plumage soft, furry, waterproof, brown above, lighter below. Sexes alike.

Habits: Rather weak fliers, but strong, agile swimmers. Swim entirely with feet; steer with feet in flight. Eat fish and other aquatic animals. Nest, a floating platform of vegetation. Eggs 3–10, white, soon stained brown. Incubation and natal care by both parents.

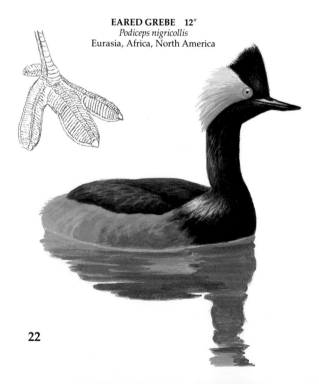

EARED GREBE   12"
Podiceps nigricollis
Eurasia, Africa, North America

TUBE-NOSED SWIMMERS—Procellariiformes

Contains 4 families of oceanic birds that rarely come to land except to breed. Occur in all the open seas of the world, but predominantly in the Southern Hemisphere. Most are fine fliers and highly migratory. Nostrils extend onto the bill in short tubes, usually on top, sometimes opening on each side. Bill covered with horny plates. Three front toes connected by webs. Good swimmers. Distinctive musty body odor. Lay a single white egg. Incubation and fledgling periods are relatively long.

ALBATROSSES, Diomedeidae

Distribution: 19 Species, 13 living, 10 fossil, earliest Middle Eocene of Nigeria. Oceans of the world except North Atlantic, Arctic, and tropical doldrums. Migratory.

Characteristics: 28–52″. Wingspread to 11′. Large, goose-size birds. Stout bill strongly hooked and plated. Nostril tubes open through side of bill. Wings very long, narrow, pointed. Some solid brown or gray; others black above, white below. Sexes alike.

Habits: Marvelous gliders that need wind to fly well; sometimes "grounded" by calms. Feed on fish, squid, plankton, refuse from ships. Nest on oceanic islands. Incubation by both sexes. Very long incubation and fledgling periods.

YELLOW-NOSED ALBATROSS 30″
Diomedea chlororhynchos
Southern oceans

SHEARWATERS AND PETRELS, Procellariidae

Distribution: 69 species, 53 living, 27 fossil, earliest Middle Oligocene of Belgium. Seas and oceans of the world. All are migratory, some highly so.

Characteristics: 11–36″. Medium-sized birds with nasal tubes on top of hooked bill. Wings long, pointed; tail short. Colored white, black, brown, gray, or combinations thereof; some have two color phases. Sexes alike.

Habits: Pelagic birds that fly mostly by gliding. Main food is fish and plankton; some eat other birds, carrion, garbage from ships. Most nest colonially in underground burrows; some on sea-cliff ledges. Incubation and natal care by both sexes.

SOOTY SHEARWATER   18″
Puffinus griseus
Oceans of the world

BLACK-CAPPED PETREL   15″
Pterodroma hasitata
Tropical Atlantic Ocean

STORM-PETRELS, Hydrobatidae

Distribution: 22 species, 20 living, 1 recently extinct, 2 fossil, earliest Upper Miocene of California. Oceans of the world except Arctic. Most are migratory.

Characteristics: 6–10″. Small birds with nasal tubes opening on top of slender, hooked, grooved bill. Wings long, pointed; tail often forked. Legs slender, rather long. Brownish-black to gray, often with a white rump. Sexes alike.

Habits: Patter over the sea with erratic, fluttering flight close to water, often in small, scattered flocks. Feed from surface on small marine animals, fatty carrion, and scraps. Nest colonially in burrows or rock crevices. Incubation and natal care by both parents.

WHITE-BELLIED STORM-PETREL   8″
Fregetta grallana
South Atlantic Ocean

WILSON'S STORM-PETREL   7″
Oceanites oceanicus
Breeds circumpolarly in Antarctica;
winters in northern oceans

FORK-TAILED STORM-PETREL
Oceanodroma furcata
North Pacific Ocean

25

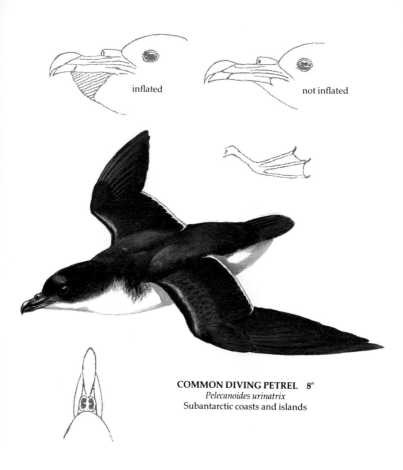

inflated

not inflated

COMMON DIVING PETREL 8″
Pelecanoides urinatrix
Subantarctic coasts and islands

DIVING PETRELS, Pelecanoididae

Distribution: 4 species, 4 living, 1 fossil from Pleistocene of Peru. Southern oceans south of latitude 35° S. Most nonmigratory.

Characteristics: 7–10″. Nasal tubes open upward on top of short, stout, hooked bill. Body chunky; neck, wings, tail, and legs short. All very similar, black above, white below; superficially resemble the auklets. Sexes alike.

Habits: Rather weak fliers, but excellent swimmers and divers. Use wings under water; often fly out of water and through waves. Food consists mainly of marine animals. Nest in burrows or under rocks in small colonies. Their breeding habits closely parallel those of the storm-petrels. Lay a single white egg. Incubation and natal care by both sexes.

**ROCKHOPPER
PENGUIN 25"**
Eudyptes crestatus
Subantarctic islands

PENGUINS—Sphenisciformes

Contains a single family of flightless swimming birds.

PENGUINS, Spheniscidae

Distribution: 48 species, 15 living, 36 fossil, earliest from Lower Eocene of New Zealand. Southern Hemisphere islands, coasts, and waters. Some migratory.

Characteristics: 16–50". Short legs; heavy webbed feet far back on body. Paddle-like wings do not fold; no flight feathers; tail short. Plumage thick, waterproof; apteria small. Dark above, lighter below.

Habits: Flightless, but swim superbly, propel with wings, steer with feet. Eat fish, shrimp, squid. Nest on ground or in burrow. Eggs 1–2; incubation by both sexes; in Emperor Penguin largely by male on top of his feet on Antarctic shelf ice.

FULL-WEBBED SWIMMERS—Pelecaniformes

Contains 6 living and 6 extinct families of fish-eating birds found on or near water in temperate and tropical regions throughout the world. The only birds with all four toes connected by webs. Most living forms have large wings, short legs, bill as long or longer than the

RED-TAILED TROPICBIRD   19/35"
Phaethon rubricauda
Tropical Indian and Pacific Oceans

TROPICBIRDS, Phaethontidae

Distribution: 4 species, 3 living, 2 fossil, earliest Lower Eocene of England. Tropic and subtropic seas of the world. Partly migratory.

Characteristics: 16–19" (without central tail feathers, which sometimes measure 20" more). Bill long, pointed, slightly downcurved. Wings long, pointed; legs short; feet small. White with black on head and wings. Sexes alike.

Habits: Strong fliers, but swim poorly and can barely walk. Dive on fish and squid from a height. Build no nest; lay single buffy egg, spotted black, on cliff ledges. Both sexes incubate and rear downy young.

head, nasal openings almost or entirely blocked, and a more or less expandable throat pouch.

Living forms fly strongly (one flightless); most swim well but walk poorly. Most are migratory. Build a flimsy nest or none at all. Lay 1–6 chalky eggs. Altricial young hatch blind, usually naked; both parents feed them by regurgitation for 5–8 weeks before they fledge.

PELICANS, Pelecanidae

Distribution: 16 species, 6 living, 15 fossil, earliest Lower Miocene of France. Temperate and tropical coasts and large inland lakes of both hemispheres. Some migratory.

Characteristics: 50–72". Bill very long, hooked, with enormous gular pouch. Wings broad; legs short, stout; feet large, strong. Neck long, tail short. One species brown, others white with black wingtips. Sexes alike.

Habits: Strong fliers; soar well. Feed from surface or by diving from a height, scooping up fish in pouch. Nest in colonies, sometimes of immense size. Eggs 1–4 in tree or ground nest. Natal care is provided by both sexes.

AUSTRALIAN PELICAN   65"
Pelecanus conspicillatus
Australia, southern New Guinea

BOOBIES AND GANNETS, Sulidae

Distribution: 25 species, 7 living, 22 fossil, earliest Lower Oligocene of France. Tropic and temperate oceans of the world except N. Pacific. High latitude species migratory, others move locally.

Characteristics: 26–40″. Large birds with long, pointed wings, stout pointed bill. Legs short; feet large. Small gular pouch; bare skin of throat and face often highly colored. Adults white and black or brown; young, brown. Sexes similar, female usually larger.

Habits: Usually gregarious. Strong fliers alternating rapid wingbeats with glides. Dive into water from a height; also pursue fish under water. Nest colonially on ledges or trees. Natal chores by both sexes.

†PELAGORNIS, Pelagornithidae

1 species, known by a humerus from the Miocene of France.

†CLADORNIS, Cladornithidae

1 species, by leg bones found in the Oligocene of Argentina.

†CYPHORNIS, Cyphornithidae

3 species by Lower Miocene leg bones, *Cyphornis* from British Columbia; *Palaeochenoides* and *Tympanonesiotes* from South Carolina.

NORTHERN GANNET 40″
Sula bassanus
Coasts of North Atlantic, S. Africa, Australia, New Zealand

SPOTTED SHAG
39″
Phalacrocorax
punctatus
New Zealand

GREAT CORMORANT   40″
Phalacrocorax carbo
Almost cosmopolitan

CORMORANTS, Phalacrocoracidae

Distribution: 55 species, 29 living, 1 recently extinct, 33 fossil, earliest Upper Paleocene of New Jersey. Worldwide except western Pacific islands; on tropic and temperate coasts, rivers, lakes, swamps. Northern forms migratory.

Characteristics: 19–40″. Body, neck, tail elongate; short legs at end of body; long, thin tubular bill hooked strongly at tip. Northern species blackish; Southern Hemisphere forms grayish or with white underparts. Head is often crested. Sexes similar.

Habits: Usually gregarious. Fly close to water with steady wingbeats. After swimming, sit with wings spead to dry. Dive from surface and chase fish, amphibians, and crustacea under water. Both sexes build nest, incubate and rear young. Galapagos Cormorant flightless.

†ELOPTERYX, Elopterygidae

3 primitive water birds showing affinities to both the boobies and the cormorants. *Elopteryx* known from leg bones from Upper Cretaceous of Rumania; *Argillornis* by wing bone fragments from Eocene of England, Belgium; *Eostega* by mandible from Middle Eocene of Rumania.

ANHINGAS, Anhingidae

Distribution: 7 species, 2 living, 6 fossil, earliest Middle Eocene of Sumatra. North and South America, southern Africa, southern Asia, Australia, New Zealand; in fresh-water lakes, swamps, rivers, estuaries. North American species migratory.

Characteristics: 34–36″. Strongly resemble cormorants, but body, head, neck more slender; bill sharply pointed. Short legs placed far back. Males are black with white on neck and wings; females have light brown head and neck.

Habits: Somewhat gregarious. Fly strongly, soar well. Often swim with only head and neck above water. After swimming sit with wings spread to dry. Chase fish, amphibians, crustacea under water and spear prey with bill. Breed colonially; build bulky nest in trees over or near water. Natal chores by both sexes.

ANHINGA 36″
Anhinga anhinga
SE U.S., Central and S. America

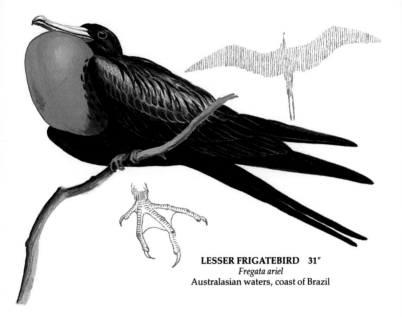

LESSER FRIGATEBIRD   31"
Fregata ariel
Australasian waters, coast of Brazil

†ODONTOPTERYX, Odontopterygidae

1 species, a large sea bird with toothlike serrations in its bill, known by a skull from the Lower Eocene of England.

†PSEUDONTORNIS, Pseudontornithidae

2 species, *Pseudontornis* from a Miocene skull of uncertain locality, Brazil or Germany, and *Osteodontornis* from a Miocene skeletal impression from California.

FRIGATEBIRDS, Fregatidae

Distribution: 5 species, 5 living, 1 fossil from Quaternary deposits. Tropical seas and oceanic islands the world around. Nonmigratory but wander locally.

Characteristics: 30–40". Wings very long, narrow, pointed; tail long, forked; bill long, hooked. Legs very short; feet small. Throat bare, distendible and red in male. Brownish-black; white underparts in some. Sexes usually unlike, female larger.

Habits: Gregarious. Most expert of fliers, light, graceful on wing, but almost helpless on land or in water. Feed from sea surface while hovering; rob pelicans, boobies, gulls of fish. Nest on trees or rock ledges; female brings material, male builds nest; both sexes incubate and rear young.

33

HERONS AND ALLIES—Ciconiiformes

Contains 1 fossil and 5 living families of long-legged, long-necked wading birds occurring in almost all ice-free lands of the world. All have broad, rounded wings and four long, spreading toes, the front three in some families slightly webbed at the base. Plumage varies from dull to

HERONS, Ardeidae

Distribution: 81 species, 63 living, 1 recently extinct, 35 fossil, earliest Lower Eocene of England. Worldwide in temperate and tropical regions in swamps, marshes, and along shores. Temperate forms migratory.

Characteristics: 12–56". Wings large, rounded. Bill long, straight, pointed. Lores bare; tibia partly bare. Middle claw with comb. Have powder downs. Loose, soft plumage in simple patterns of grays, blues, browns; some pure white. Sexes similar.

Habits: Flight strong, direct, with neck drawn in. Solitary or gregarious. Many nocturnal or crepuscular. Feed on aquatic animals , mainly by wading, stalking or patient waiting, usually in shallows; eat some insects. Eggs 3–7 in flimsy shallow nest in trees, bushes, or on ground. Female builds nest but both sexes incubate and care for downy, nidicolous young.

PURPLE HERON   31"
Ardea purpurea
Southern Eurasia to Phillippines, Africa, Madagascar

**BLACK-CROWNED
NIGHT-HERON   28"**
Nycticorax nycticorax
Almost cosmopolitan
in temperate and tropical regions

bright; simple patterns. Sexes alike or nearly so. Most are strong fliers. May be gregarious or solitary. All are carnivorous, food is mainly fish, amphibians, reptiles, crustaceans, also some insects and carrion. Eggs 1–6, usually white or bluish. Both parents incubate and rear the altricial young in the nest.

†PLEGADORNIS, Plegadornithidae

1 species, a primitive ibis known by part of a left humerus from the Upper Cretaceous of Alabama.

IBISES AND SPOONBILLS, Threskiornithidae

Distribution: 35 species, 28 living, 15 fossil, earliest Upper Eocene of England. Worldwide in varied temperate and tropical habitats.

Characteristics: 20–40". Bill long, slender and downcurved or broadly spatulate. Neck and legs moderately long. Front toes webbed at base. Plumage usually plain white, brown, or black (1 pink, 1 red).

Habits: Mostly gregarious. Flight direct with neck outstretched. Fly in regular lines; often circle and soar. Voices harsh. Food largely aquatic animals, some seeds and vegetable matter. Nest of sticks, rushes, on trees, cliffs, or marshy ground. Eggs 2–5, white or blue, plain or spotted. Downy young reared in nest by both parents.

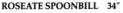

ROSEATE SPOONBILL   34"
Ajaia ajaja.
S. U.S., West Indies to Argentina and Chile

SCARLET IBIS   27"
Eudocimus ruber
Venezuela to Brazil

WHITE STORK 40"
Ciconia ciconia
Eurasia

STORKS, Ciconiidae

Distribution: 40 species, 17 living, 29 fossil, earliest Upper Eocene of France. Temperate Eurasia through Africa; n. Australia; s.e. United States through South America. Habitat varied, usually near water. Northern species migratory.

Characteristics: 28–60". Wings long, broad; tail short, usually rounded. Body heavy; neck rather long; bill large, heavy, variously shaped. Legs very long; front toes partly webbed. Usually boldly black and white or all black or white. Face or head bare in some. Sexes alike.

Habits: Somewhat gregarious, diurnal birds. Fly strongly with neck out straight; soar well and often. Have courtship dance.Nearly voiceless, but rattle bill. Eggs 3–5, in a stick platform nest on tree, cliff ledge, or building. Young nidicolous.

HAMMERHEAD, Scopidae

Distribution: 1 species; s.w. Arabia, tropical Africa, Madagascar; in broken woodlands, grasslands, usually near water. Nonmigratory.

Characteristics: 20". Head anvil-shaped, with long crest and large hooked bill. Neck and legs rather short, toes long. No powder downs. Sexes alike.

Habits: Usually in pairs or small flocks. Fly slowly with neck out straight. Crepuscular. Voice harsh. Fond of awkward gamboling. Eggs 3–6, white, in large domed, intricately compartmented nest. Downy young nidicolous.

SHOEBILL (or WHALEHEAD) STORK, Balaenicipitidae

Distribution: 1 species; Africa, from southern Sudan to northern Uganda and eastern Zaire in riverine marshes. Nonmigratory.

Characteristics: 47". Large, stork-like bird with a grotesque, swollen, hooked beak it carries on its breast. Single pair of powder downs. Sexes alike.

Habits: Usually solitary, morose, sluggish, but wary. Flies with neck drawn in. Clatters bill. Eats fish, amphibians, reptiles. Eggs 2 in ground nest. Young nidicolous.

HAMMERHEAD   20"
Scopus umbretta
Arabia, Africa, Madagascar

SHOEBILL STORK   47"
Balaeniceps rex
Africa, upper White Nile
to Shaba and Uganda

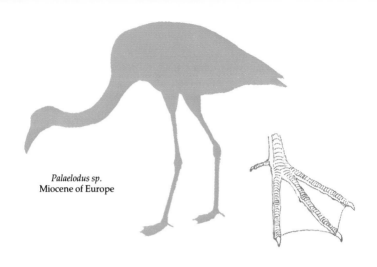

Palaelodus sp.
Miocene of Europe

FLAMINGOS AND ANCESTORS—
Phoenicopteriformes

Contains 5 fossil families and 1 living family of wading birds that show structural and behavioral affinities to both the herons and the waterfowl.

†TOROTIX, Torotigidae

3 species known by a few Lower Cretaceous wing or leg bones; *Gallornis* from France, *Parascaniornis* from Sweden, and *Torotix* from Wyoming.

†SCANIORNIS, Scaniornithidae

1 species, known by a humerus, a coracoid, and a scapula from the Lower Paleocene of Sweden.

†TELMABATES, Telmabatidae

1 species, known by a post-cranial skeleton from the Lower Eocene of Argentina.

†AGNOPTERUS, Agnopteridae

3 species, each known by only a few bones, 2 from Upper Eocene of France and England, 1 from Oligocene of Kazakstan.

†PALAELODUS, Palaelodidae

8 species; 6 *Palaelodus* from Miocene of Europe; 2 *Megapaloedus* from Miocene and Pliocene of South Dakota, California, Oregon.

FLAMINGOS, Phoenicopteridae

Distribution: 16 species, 4 living, 14 fossil, earliest Upper Eocene of England. Africa, Madagascar, India, s. Europe, Caribbean coasts, Andean highlands, Galapagos; in shallow lagoons, lakes, estuaries; fresh, brackish, and salt water. Some migratory.

Characteristics: 36–50″. Wading birds with enormously long neck and legs. Bill unique, bent abruptly downward in middle; upper bill moves, lower almost rigid. Tongue thick. Front toes webbed. Wings long, strong; tail short. Solidly white to pink; flight feathers black. Sexes similar.

Habits: Gregarious. Fly strongly with neck extended, in irregular lines or V's. Food, minute animal and vegetable matter sieved from mud pumped through bill by thick, muscular tongue. Swim well when necessary. Nest a mud cone; eggs 1–2, white. Incubation and care of nidifugous young by both sexes.

GREATER FLAMINGO   45–50″
Phoenicopterus ruber
West Indies, South America, Eurasia, Africa

WATERFOWL—Anseriformes

A group of semiaquatic birds composed of 2 strongly marked families. Practically comopolitan except for Antarctica and the frozen Arctic Ocean. All swim well and most are strong fliers. Relatively short-legged, long-

SCREAMERS, Anhimidae

Distribution: 3 species, 3 living, 1 fossil from Quaternary of Argentina. Venezuela and Colombia s. to Uruguay and n. Argentina; in marshes, lagoons, ponds, wet grasslands. Nonmigratory.

Characteristics: 28–36″. Heavy bodied; head crested or spiked; bill fowl-like; legs heavy; large feet partly webbed; 2 prominent spurs at bend of wing. Many subcutaneous air sacs; skeleton highly pneumatic. Black to gray above, lighter below; sexes alike.

Habits: Somewhat gregarious. Semiaquatic. Fly strongly but slowly; often soar for hours. Walk on floating vegetation; swim well; sometimes perch in trees. Voices loud, shrill. Food vegetable, largely succculent aquatic plants. Eggs 1–6, white, in grass nest on marshy ground. Natal care by both sexes; downy young nidifugous.

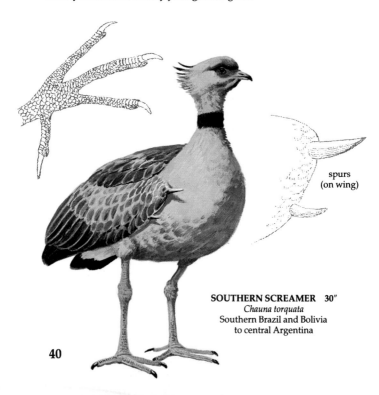

spurs
(on wing)

SOUTHERN SCREAMER   30″
Chauna torquata
Southern Brazil and Bolivia
to central Argentina

necked, full-bodied birds, they have 11 primaries (the first greatly reduced in length), rounded open nostrils, and a feathered oil gland. Adults have an undercoat of down feathers and lack an incubation patch. The eggs are never marked, and the downy young are nidifugous.

WATERFOWL, Anatidae

Distribution: 245 species, 148 living, 4 recently extinct, 177 fossil, earliest Middle Eocene of Utah. Worldwide except polar regions, in highly varied habitats, usually near water. Most species migratory.

Characteristics: 12–60″. Bill flat, wide, rounded at end, with combed serrations at edges. Legs short; 3 front toes fully webbed. Neck medium to long; wings narrow and pointed; tail short. Widely variable in form, size, color; sexes either alike or unlike.

Habits: Usually gregarious swimming birds that fly strongly and rapidly (a few flightless) and walk well. Food quite diverse, both vegetable and animal. Nesting behavior varied; nest on ground or in trees, often lined with female's breast feathers. Eggs 2–16. One species parasitic.

†EONESSA, Eonessinae

A single fossil species known from a few wing bones from the Eocene of Utah.

†ROMAINVILLIA, Romainvilliinae

A single fossil species known from wing and leg bones from the Oligocene of France.

†PARANYROCA, Paranyrocinae

A fossil pochard known from leg bone from the Lower Miocene of South Dakota.

Paranyroca magna
Miocene of South Dakota

Eonessa anaticula
Eocene of Utah

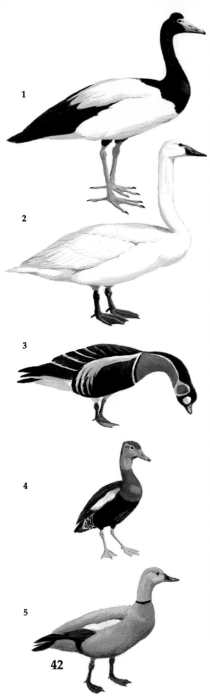

PIED GEESE, Anseranatinae
A single long-legged Australian species that shows affinities to the screamers. **(1)**

SWANS, Cygnini
6 species of large white (one black) birds with long graceful necks that are longer than the body. **(2)**

GEESE, Anserinae
14 species of large-bodied birds of high latitudes; long necks but necks are shorter than the body. **(3)**

WHISTLING-DUCKS,
Dendrocygnini
8 species of long-legged ducks of warm-temperate and tropical distribution. **(4)**

SHELDRAKES, Tadornini
20 large, somewhat goose-like ducks, often with boldly, brightly colored, thick bills. **(5)**

PERCHING DUCKS,
Cairinini
12 species of essentially forest ducks that perch in trees and have long, sharp claws. **(6)**

TORRENT DUCKS,
Merganettini
Little-known inhabitants of rushing Andean mountain streams. A single species with several races. **(7)**

DABBLING DUCKS,
Anatinae
41 species of largely familiar fresh-water ducks. Have a simple hind toe with a nail. **(8)**

POCHARDS, Aythyini
16 species of heavy-bodied bay ducks. Have feet wide apart, and a hind toe flap. **(9)**

42

SEA DUCKS, Mergini

20 species. Fine swimmers and divers. Bill with serrate edges. **(10)**

STIFF-TAILED DUCKS, Oxyurini

9 species. Small ducks with feet well back. Swim well. **(11)**

1. **PIED GOOSE** 35″
   Anseranas semipalmata
   Australia

2. **TUNDRA SWAN** 50″
   Cygnus columbianus
   Circumpolar in
   Northern Hemisphere

3. **RED-BREASTED GOOSE** 22″
   Branta ruficollis
   North-central Siberia

4. **BLACK-BELLIED WHISTLING-DUCK** 20″
   Dendrocygna autumnalis
   Texas to Argentina

5. **RUDDY SHELDRAKE** 25″
   Tadorna ferruginea
   Northern Asia, northeast Africa

6. **MANDARIN DUCK** 20″
   Aix galericulata
   East Asia and Japan

7. **TORRENT DUCK** 17″
   Merganetta armata
   Andes, Venezuela
   to Tierra del Fuego

8. **SILVER TEAL** 15″
   Anas versicolor
   South Brazil, Argentina, Chile

9. **REDHEAD** 22″
   Aythya americana
   North America

10. **COMMON EIDER** 24″
    Somateria mollissima
    Circumpolar in
    Northern Hemisphere

11. **RUDDY DUCK** 17″
    Oxyura jamaicensis
    North America,
    n. South America,
    West Indies

BIRDS OF PREY—Falconiformes

Contains 1 fossil and 4 living families of predators. Bill strong and sharply hooked, with fleshy cere across the top through which the nostrils open. Legs and feet stout; claws long and sharp; hind toe opposable. Wings large,

†NEOCATHARTES, Neocathartidae

1 species, known from a partial skeleton from the Eocene of Wyoming. A peculiarly long-legged vulture.

AMERICAN VULTURES, Cathartidae

Distribution: 24 species, 7 living, 24 fossil, earliest from Eocene and Oliogocene of Europe. *Teratornis*, from Pleistocene of California and Nevada, largest flying bird that ever lived. Temperate and tropical America in forests, grasslands, brushlands, deserts, mountains. High latitude populations migratory.

Characteristics: 25–52″. Bill heavy, rounded, hooked; wings long, broad; tail medium to long; legs of medium length; toes long, claws weak. Head and neck bare; plumage usually black or brown (one species white and black); sexes alike.

Habits: Great soarers. Usually solitary but flock where food is plentiful. Voracious consumers of carrion and animal refuse; seldom attack living prey. Nature of food makes them ill-smelling. Disgorge when disturbed. Usually no nest as such; eggs 1–3, in cave, tree hollow, or on cliff ledge.

LESSER YELLOW-HEADED VULTURE 24″
Cathartes burrovianus
Mexico to northern Argentina

Neocathartes grallator
Eocene of Wyoming

rounded or pointed. Plumage variable, but sexes usually similar; female larger than male. Powerful, strong-winged fliers that live almost entirely on animal food. Nesting varied but reproductive rate is low; clutches small; incubation and rearing periods long.

SECRETARY BIRD 46″
Sagittarius serpentarius
Africa south of the Sahara

SECRETARY BIRD, Sagittariidae

Distribution: 1 living species, 2 fossils from Eocene and Miocene of France. Africa south of the Sahara in open dry plains. Partially migratory; much local movement.

Characteristics; 46″. Legs long; toes short, front ones partly webbed; claws long, sharp, downcurved. Crest of plumes on back of head; central tail feathers very long. Body gray. Flight feathers and thighs black. Sexes alike; male slightly larger.

Habits: Solitary, usually in pairs. Fly seldom but well. Hunt on foot; run when disturbed. Food largely reptiles, also large insects, small mammals and birds. Roost in trees or large bushes. Bulky nest of sticks and sods in bush or low tree, used year after year. Eggs 2–3, bluish-white, incubated by female; male helps feed young.

HAWKS, EAGLES, KITES, HARRIERS, OLD WORLD VULTURES, Accipitridae

Distribution: 273 species, 205 living, 118 fossil, back to Eocene of Europe. Worldwide except for Antarctica and some oceanic islands. Habitat widely varied. Temperate zone forms migratory.

Characteristics: 10–45". Wings broad, rounded; legs medium; feet strong; claws hooked. Tail medium to long; neck short. Cere and eye ring bare, often brightly colored. Plumage varied, mostly browns and grays, often barred or streaked. Sexes similar; female usually larger.

Habits: Solitary as a rule, but some migrate in loose flocks. Flight strong, often soaring. Hunt live prey of all sorts, pouncing on it and killing it with talons. Voices usually loud whistles or screams. Nest of sticks or grasses, in trees or cliffs or on ground. Eggs 1–6, white, clear or marked with brown. Natal care by both parents.

WHITE-TAILED KITES, Elaninae

7 species of light-colored raptors with an airy, graceful flight, of temperate-tropical distribution. **(1)**

HONEY BUZZARDS, Perninae

13 species of long-winged, long-tailed kites, includes Swallow-tailed and Hook-billed Kites. **(2)**

TRUE KITES, Milvinae

Poorly marked group of 14 species connecting Perninae and Accipitrinae. Contains Mississippi, Plumbeous, and Snail Kites. **(3)**

1. **BLACK-SHOULDERED KITE   16"**
   Elanus caeruleus
   Southern U.S. to Argentina
2. **SWALLOW-TAILED KITE   24"**
   Elanoides forficatus
   Southern U.S. to n. Argentina
3. **RED KITE   24"**
   Milvus milvus
   Europe, northern Africa

GOSHAWKS, Accipitrinae

Some 40 species of hunting hawks with long legs, rounded wings. Live largely on small birds and mammals. **(4)**

TRUE HAWKS AND EAGLES, Buteoninae

Some 90 species of broad-winged soaring hawks, found worldwide. Most familiar species belong here. **(5)**

OLD WORLD VULTURES, Aegypiinae

14 species of Old World carrion-eaters; Egyptian, Griffon, and Hooded Vultures. **(6)**

HARRIERS, Circinae

17 species of slender, long-winged, long-tailed birds with prominent facial disc. Cosmopolitan in open land. **(7)**

SERPENT EAGLES, Circaetinae

13 fairly large, broad-winged hawks of the Old World, fond of soaring over marshy areas, live largely on reptiles. **(8)**

4. **NORTHERN GOSHAWK   26"**
   Accipiter gentilis
   Temperate Northern Hemisphere
5. **GOLDEN EAGLE   33"**
   Aquila chrysaetos
   Temperate Northern Hemisphere
6. **LAMMERGEIER   45"**
   Gypaetus barbatus
   Southern Eurasia to southern Africa
7. **PIED HARRIER   17"**
   Circus melanoleucus
   Manchuria to Ceylon and Borneo
8. **BANDED SNAKE EAGLE   24"**
   Circaetus fasciolatus
   Tanzania to Natal

OSPREYS, Acciptridae, Pandioninae

Distribution: 1 living species known from Pleistocene of Europe and North America. Almost cosmopolitan, on seashores, inland lakes, and rivers. Most populations migratory.

Characteristics: 24″. Wings broad, somewhat pointed; legs stout with small, rough scales; undersurface of feet with sharp spicules; outer toe reversible. Dark brown above, white below; tail barred. Sexes alike.

Habits: Usually solitary; sometimes nest in loose colonies, always near water. Feed almost entirely on fish; hunt over open water, plunge from a height down often completely under water to grasp fish with claws. Carry fish head foremost in both feet to perch or nest. Nest massive; on tree or ground. Eggs 2–4, incubated mainly by female, to whom male brings food at nest.

OSPREY 24″
Pandion haliaetus
Almost cosmopolitan
in temperate and tropical regions

FALCONS, Falconidae

Distribution: 69 species, 57 living, 1 recently extinct, 11 fossil, earliest Miocene of Argentina. Worldwide except for Antarctica and oceanic islands. Habitat varied; some species migratory.

Characteristics: 6–25″. Wings long, pointed; bill short, hooked, usually notched. Neck short; legs medium to long; toes and claws strong, hooked; cere and eye ring bare. Vary widely in color, usually subdued hues. Sexes usually similar; female larger.

Habits: Generally solitary or in pairs. Flight strong, fast; soar infrequently. Falcons capture living prey with feet; caracaras live mostly on carrion. Nest of sticks in trees or cliffs; sometimes use old nest of other species. Voice loud screams, squeaks. Eggs 2–6; incubation and natal care by both parents.

PEREGRINE FALCON   18"
Falco peregrinus
Entire Northern Hemisphere,
Australia, S. Africa, Patagonia

notched bill

CRESTED CARACARA   24"
Polyborus plancus
S. U.S. to Venezuela, Colombia,
and Peru

Caracara

Falcon

Osprey

FOWL-LIKE BIRDS—Galliformes

Contains 4 families of mainly terrestrial birds found the world around except in Antarctica and Oceania. Wings short, rounded; bill short, stout, downcurved, with overlapping tip; legs strong; feet stout; hind toe always present. Often cryptically colored; many of them are breathtakingly beautiful.

MEGAPODES, Megapodiidae

Distribution: 11 species, 10 living, 2 fossil, earliest Pleistocene of Australia. Australia, Malaya, n. to Philippines, e. to Samoa. In forests and dry scrub country. Nonmigratory.

Characteristics: 10–30″. Wings rounded; tail medium to long, vaulted in some. Legs and feet very large and strong. One species crested, others with head bare, wattled, or casqued. Solid dark brown, or streaked brown and grayish. Sexes alike.

Habits: Somewhat gregarious but shy terrestrial birds. Fly heavily when pressed to nearby low tree branches. Bury their 6–24 buffy-white eggs in sand, warm volcanic ash, or in mounds of rotting vegetation and soil for sun or other heat to incubate. Young hatch feathered and able to fly; extricate themselves from nest mound. No parental care.

AUSTRALIAN BRUSH TURKEY   30″
Alectura lathami
Eastern Australia

Terrestrial (a few arboreal) running and scratching birds. Fly fast for short distances, but swim poorly. Tend to be resident (only 4 species migratory) wherever found. Nest usually on the ground. Downy young nidifugous. All have the familiar characteristics of the chicken but their relationship to other bird orders is not clear-cut. Among the earliest to be domesticated.

WHITE-CRESTED PIPING GUAN 35″
Pipilo cumanensis
Venezuela and Ecuador to Argentina

RUFOUS-VENTED CHACHALACA 25″
Ortalis ruficauda
Colombia and Venezuela

CHACHALACAS, Cracidae (includes Guans and Curassows)

Distribution: 66 species, 38 living, 36 fossil, back to Eocene of North America and Europe. S. Texas to Argentina and Paraguay, mostly in lowland forests. Nonmigratory.

Characteristics: 20–40″. Legs bare; feet large, hind toe at same level as front ones. Tail long, flat, wide. Lores bare; throat bare and wattled in some. Some crested, a few casqued. Plain-colored fowls with glossy black or soft brown plumage, largely unpatterned.

Habits: Somewhat gregarious forest birds. Feed on ground and fly into trees when disturbed. Flight fast but labored. Calls loud and harsh. Simple nest of sticks on a tree branch. Eggs 2–5, incubated by female.

GROUSE, Phasianidae, Tetraoninae

Distribution: 28 species, 18 living, 24 fossil, earliest Miocene of North America. Circumpolar in temperate and subarctic parts of Northern Hemisphere. Nonmigratory, but some seasonal wandering.

Characteristics: 12–34″. Legs feathered, also toes in some. Tail variable, usually shorter than wing. Head sometimes with naked spots. Most are cryptically colored in browns, grays, blacks. Three species turn white in winter. Sexes alike and unlike.

Habits: Usually solitary ground-dwellers, sometimes in small bands. Feed on vegetable matter, some insects. Generally polygamous, with elaborate courtship display. Some have communal display grounds where females come to mate. Nest building, incubation, care of young by female alone. Eggs 6–16. Nest usually on ground.

WHITE-TAILED PTARMIGAN   14″
Lagopus leucurus
Western Cordilleras from
Alaska to New Mexico

COMMON HAZEL HEN   14″
Tetrastes bonasia
Temperate n. Eurasia

COMMON CAPERCAILLIE   34″
Tetrao urogallus
Forested Europe to central Siberia

52

PHEASANTS, Phasianidae, Phasianinae (includes Partridges, Grouse, Francolins, Peafowl, Turkeys, Guineafowl, Chickens, and Quails.)

Distribution: 241 species, 177 living, 1 recently extinct, 63 fossil, earliest Oligocene of Saskatchewan. Almost worldwide, except southern S.A., in temperate and tropical habitats. A few species migratory.

Characteristics: 5–78". A widely diverse family, most diagnostic features anatomical. Legs short to fairly long, strong, sometimes spurred; tarsus usually bare. Bill small, henlike. Tail very short to extremely long. Some species crested or wattled. Sexes usually unlike.

Habits: Most gregarious (a few solitary) ground-living birds. Obtain plant and animal food mostly by chicken-like scratching. Easily domesticated. New World forms generally monogamous, Old World ones polygamous. Eggs 2–22. Incubation and natal care by female alone or by both parents.

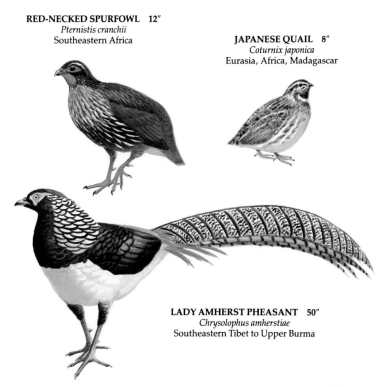

RED-NECKED SPURFOWL   12"
Pternistis cranchii
Southeastern Africa

JAPANESE QUAIL   8"
Coturnix japonica
Eurasia, Africa, Madagascar

LADY AMHERST PHEASANT   50"
Chrysolophus amherstiae
Southeastern Tibet to Upper Burma

GUINEAFOWLS, Phasianidae, Numidinae

Distribution: 7 species. Africa s. of Sahara, Madagascar; in open forest, scrub country, grasslands. Nonmigratory wanderers; travel in flocks.

Characteristics: 17–30″. Head and upper neck bare, usually with bony helmet or occipital feather patch. Bill large, stout; legs strong; feet large; tail small, drooping. Back and rump arched in contour. Plumage black, spotted and barred with white. Sexes similar. Distantly related to the pheasants.

Habits: All but 1 species highly gregarious. Essentially ground birds. Run swiftly, sometimes long distances. Flight short but powerful. Roost in trees. Wary birds with harsh, discordant, repetitive voices. Run rather than fly to escape danger. Eggs 7–20 in crude ground nest; incubation by female; natal care by both sexes.

TURKEYS, Phasianidae, Meleagridinae

Distribution: 10 species, 2 living, 10 fossil, earliest Pliocene of Kansas. East and central U.S. s. to Guatemala. Woodlands and open forests. Nonmigratory. Entirely indigenous to the New World; domesticated by the Indians in Mexico early in 16th century. Now improved by selective breeding.

Characteristics: 35–48″. Head and upper neck bare, with fleshy wattles. Body large; neck long; wings and tail broad, rounded. Legs stout, spurred. Bronzy plumage marked with black, brown, white. Sexes similar; female smaller, duller. Show similarity to pheasants but differ enough to have separate family status.

Habits: Gregarious, wary, fast running birds, fly strongly for short distances. Spend day on ground; roost in trees. Polygamous; males fight and display before assembled hens. Eggs 8–18, in crude ground nest. Incubation and natal care by female alone.

HOATZIN, Opisthocomidae

Distribution: 1 species. Northeastern South America; along wooded stream banks. Nonmigratory.

Characteristics: 24″. Pheasant-like, with long, loose crest of stiff feathers. Large, rounded wings and tail. Legs short; feet large. Muscular digestive crop; degenerate gizzard. Loose-webbed plumage ruddy brown marked with creamy white. Sexes alike. Its combination of primitive yet highly specialized characteristics lead many students today to give it ordinal rank.

Habits: Gregarious inhabitants of riverine trees and shrubs. Flight very weak, mainly gliding. Restricted in movements and range. Crude nest of sticks in shrubbery over water. Eggs 2–3. Incubation period unknown. Young seminidicolous, naked at hatching, with claws on wings for climbing, which are shed during growth. Swim well, and can dive.

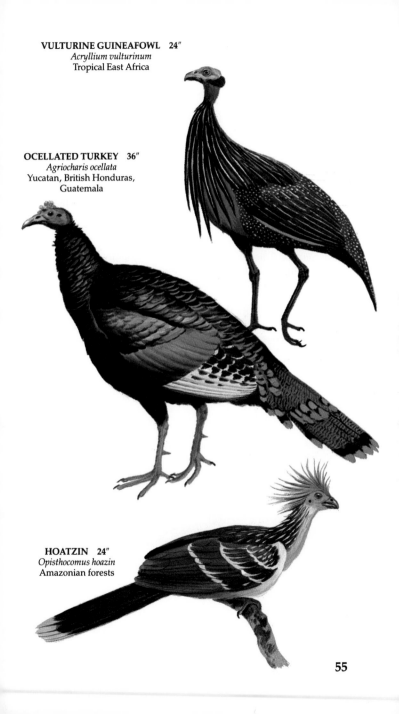

VULTURINE GUINEAFOWL   24″
Acryllium vulturinum
Tropical East Africa

OCELLATED TURKEY   36″
Agriocharis ocellata
Yucatan, British Honduras,
Guatemala

HOATZIN   24″
Opisthocomus hoazin
Amazonian forests

55

CRANES, RAILS, AND ALLIES—Gruiformes

An order of 11 living and 6 fossil families, found practically worldwide except polar regions. Most species migratory.

A varied, ancient order; diagnostic characters mainly anatomical. Variable in form and color. Crop absent.

ROATELOS, Mesitornithidae

Distribution: 3 species, Madagascar; in forests, brush country. Nonmigratory.

Characteristics: 10–11". Bill slender; wings short, rounded; tail broad, long, rounded; strong legs, feet. Mostly brownish-gray. Sexes alike and unlike.

Habits: Somewhat gregarious; usually travel in small flocks with males predominating. Largely terrestrial. Run well; fly only when forced. Run or walk with frequent stops and changes of direction. Food insects, seeds, fruit. Eggs 1–3.

†ERGILORNIS, Ergilornithidae

Three species known from leg bones: *Proergilornis* and *Ergilornis* from Oligocene of Mongolia, *Urmiornis* from Pliocene of Ukrania and Iran.

ROATELO   10"
Mesoenas unicolor
Eastern Madagascar

Hind toe elevated or level. Toes slightly or (usually) not webbed.

Either large, strong flying birds of open marshes and prairies, or weak flying (some flightless) dwellers of swampy marshes. All fly with neck straight out in front, and feet usually trailing behind. Young nidifugous. Sexes are usually alike.

HEMIPODES, Turnicidae

Distribution: 15 species. Southern Eurasia, Africa, Madagascar, Philippines, and Solomons to Australia. Open forests and grasslands. Most nonmigratory.

Characteristics: 5–8″. Wings short, rounded; tail short, soft. Toes three. Quail-like brown marked with gray and black. Sexes similar; female larger and brighter colored.

Habits: Usually singly or in pairs. Shy running birds; fly seldom, for short distances. Courtship by female. Male incubates; rears young.

COLLARED HEMIPODE, Pedionomidae

Distribution: 1 species, Australia; on open plains. Partly migratory.

Characteristics: 6½″. Similar to previous family, but toes four; legs larger; bill weaker; weak fliers. Recent studies show this strange bird may belong more properly in the Charadriiformes (page 66).

Habits: Solitary, shy, ground birds. Eggs 4; incubation by male.

BARRED BUTTON QUAIL 5-6″
Turnix suscitator
Southeastern Asia

PLAINS WANDERER 6″
Pedionomus torquatus
Southeastern Australia

†CUNAMPAIA, Cunampaiidae

One fossil species known from various bones from the Lower Oligocene of Argentina.

†IDIORNIS, Idiornithidae

4 species of *Idiornis* and 4 of *Elaphrocnemis* described from leg bones of Eocene and Oligocene of France and Wyoming.

†GASTORNIS, Gastornithidae

3 species of *Gastornis*, 1 of *Remiornis*, 1 of *Dasornis*, all from Paleocene of England and eastern Europe.

†DIATRYMA, Diatrymidae

4 species of large, fearsome, predatory, flightless ground birds from the Eocene of North America and Europe.

†PHORUSRHACOS, Phorusrhacidae

10 species of large, cursorial, Tertiary predators, earliest *Phyornis* of Argentinian Oligocene, most recent *Titanis* of Florida Pleistocene.

Diatryma sp.
Eocene of North America

COMMON WATER RAIL 11″
Rallus aquaticus
Eurasian marshlands

CORN CRAKE 10″
Crex crex
Eurasian meadowlands

PURPLE GALLINULE 13″
Porphyrula martinica
Southern U.S. to n. Argentina

RAILS, COOTS, GALLINULES, Rallidae

Distribution: 196 species, 120 living, 12 lately extinct, 91 fossil, back to Upper Cretaceous of New Jersey. Cosmopolitan except for polar regions. In marshes, wet forests, reedy streams, ponds.

Characteristics: 5–20″. Small to medium-sized birds with narrow bodies, long, strong legs and toes, longish necks, small heads.Wings rounded. Toes lobate-webbed in coots. Frontal shield in coots, gallinules. Somber brown to black or blues, often barred, spotted, striped.

Habits: Mostly solitary, a few gregarious, wading or swimming birds. Call at night. Some rails flightless, some terrestrial. Eggs 2–15, incubated by both sexes. Young highly precocious.

59

FINFOOTS OR SUNGREBES, Heliornithidae

Distribution: 3 species. Tropical Asia, Sumatra, Africa, Central and South America. On wooded streams, lakes, or watery marshes. Nonmigratory.

Characteristics: 12–24″. Body elongate; plumage close and ralline. Neck long; legs short; toes lobate-webbed. Tail long, stiff, rounded. Brownish above, lighter below; male usually larger and brighter.

Habits: Solitary, shy, secretive birds. Act like anhingas. Perch on branches over water. Swim and dive well. Fly heavily, close to water. Food fish, crustaceans, frogs, seeds, leaves. Eggs 2–7. Young cared for by male, who carries them in skin pouches under wing.

AFRICAN FINFOOT   24″
Podica senegalensis
Africa south of the Sahara

KAGU   22″
Rhynochetos jubatus
New Caledonia

KAGU , Rhynochetidae

Distribution: 1 species, New Caledonia; in forest lands near stagnant still waters and in rocky ravines. Nonmigratory.

Characteristics: 22″. Heron-like with large crested head, short neck, long legs. Plumage loose, ashy-gray above, barred with brown and dark gray. Sexes similar.

Habits: Solitary, largely nocturnal. Almost flightless; runs quickly, then stops and stands still. Food worms, insects, amphibians, mollusks. Has grotesque dance. Eggs 1, incubated by both sexes.

SUNBITTERN 18″
Eurypyga helias
S. Mexico to Brazil, N. Bolivia

CRESTED SERIEMA 36″
Cariama cristata
Tablelands of Brazil, N. Argentina

SUNBITTERN, Eurypygidae

Distribution: 1 species. Southern Mexico to Peru and central Brazil in wooded edges of streams, ponds. Nonmigratory.

Characteristics: 20″. Wings broad; tail long, broad. Bill long, sharp-pointed. Neck long, thin; legs and toes rather long. Plumage soft; variegated and barred, mottled. Sexes alike.

Habits: Semi-arboreal wading birds of wet forests; solitary. Slender, graceful. Walk slowly; fly into trees when alarmed. Dance and display with outspread wings, tail. Eggs 2, gray. Incubation by both parents.

SERIEMAS, Cariamidae

Distribution: 17 species, 2 living, 17 fossils, to Oligocene of North America. Living forms in central Brazil, Paraguay, northern Argentina; in pampas, grasslands, brush forest. Nonmigratory.

Characteristics: 32–36″. Wings short, rounded; tail long. Bill short, broad, decurved. Legs long; feet small, semipalmate. Erectile crest. Plumage soft, hairy on neck. Brownish-gray above, lighter below, finely barred. Sexes alike or nearly so.

Habits: In pairs or small flocks; stalk slowly about until disturbed, then run fast with head down. Fly weakly when pressed. Food largely ants, reptiles, berries, fruit. Eggs 2–3, in stick nest in tree or bush. Cared for by both sexes.

LIMPKINS, Aramidae

Distribution: 6 species, 1 living, 6 fossil, back to Oligocene of Argentina. Georgia, Florida, Cuba, Hispaniola, Central America south to Argentina; found in reedy marshes and swampy forests. Nonmigratory.

Characteristics: 24″. Wings short, broad, rounded. Long legs; long neck. Bill long and strong. Toes long; claws long and sharp. Brown, streaked with white. Sexes alike.

Habits: Solitary or in family groups. Walk fast but haltingly. Fly slowly for short ways with legs dangling. Loud wailing cries. Food mostly mollusks. Roost in trees. Eggs 4–8. Incubation and natal care by both sexes.

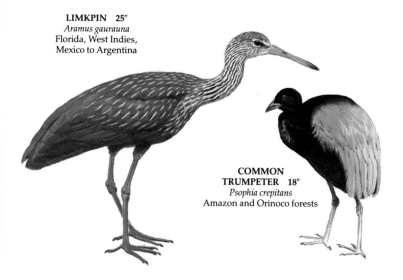

LIMKPIN 25″
Aramus gaurauna
Florida, West Indies,
Mexico to Argentina

**COMMON
TRUMPETER 18″**
Psophia crepitans
Amazon and Orinoco forests

TRUMPETERS, Psophidae

Distribution: 3 species. Amazon and Orinoco drainages in n. South America. Lowland rain forests. Nonmigratory.

Characteristics: 17–20″. Plumage soft; head and neck velvety. Bill short, stout. Legs long; neck medium. Hind toe short, elevated. Tail stumpy. Mostly black with bronzy or greenish sheen; wing feathers white, gray, or brown.

Habits: Sociable, forest-frequenting birds. Feed on forest floor; nest and roost in trees. Eat insects, fallen fruit. Carriage "humped" like guineafowl. Voice a loud, far-carrying trumpeting by male only. Eggs 6–10, white or greenish, plain. Incubated by female. Downy young nidifugous.

CRANES, Gruidae

Distribution: 43 species, 14 living, 36 fossil, earliest Eocene of Wyoming, Worldwide except South America, Malayan Arch., Oceania, New Zealand. Northern species migratory, others less so.

Characteristics: 30–60". Large, long-necked, long-legged birds, superficially resembling storks and herons, but all terrestrial, never perch in trees. Bill long, straight. Plumage largely white, gray, or brown. Sexes alike.

Habits: Conspicuous inhabitants of plains, prairies, marshes, seashores. Fly with neck straight out, feet trailing astern. Omnivorous. Loud voice. Spectacular courtship dance. Eggs usually 2; nest on ground. Both sexes incubate and rear young.

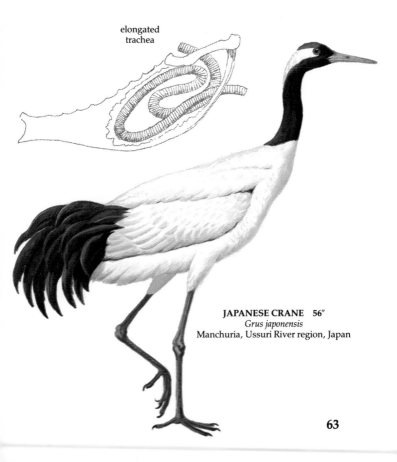

elongated trachea

JAPANESE CRANE   56"
Grus japonensis
Manchuria, Ussuri River region, Japan

BUSTARDS, Otidae

Distribution: 27 species, 23 living, 6 fossil, to Eocene of Germany. Africa, central and southern Eurasia, Australia. Open plains, brushlands. Some migratory.

Characteristics: 15–52″. Height 1 to 4½′. Large, bulky birds with long necks, stout legs, no hind toe. Bill usually short, blunt, flattened. Keen sighted. Wings broad; tail short. Buffy-brown to gray above, white to black below; some crested. Sexes unlike in color; males larger. Giant bustard of South Africa is heaviest of all flying birds.

Habits: Rather gregarious, shy, running birds. Some fly strongly with neck and legs outstretched; travel in flocks. Depend on running to escape their enemies. Never alight in trees. Omnivorous. Male has showy posturing and strutting display. Eggs 1–5 in ground nest; color of eggs varies from reddish-brown to olive green. Incubation and care of young by female. Downy young nidicolous.

DENHAM'S BUSTARD 50″
Neotis denhami
Africa south of the Sahara

Ichthyornis sp.
Cretaceous of Kansas

†ICHTHYORNIS—Ichthyornithiformes

A fossil order of 2 primitive families dating to Cretaceous time. Probably fish-eaters (Ichthyornis = fish bird), they had a well-developed keel and wing bones and thus were undoubtedly capable of fairly strong flight as we know it today. Whether they had teeth, as long believed, is not known.

†ICHTHYORNIS, Ichthyornithidae

7 species of gull-like birds from the Upper Cretaceous of Kansas and Texas. They were smallish birds standing about 8 inches high.

†APATORNIS, Apatornithidae

2 gull-like Upper Cretaceous species, one from Kansas and one from Wyoming. Their weakened shoulder bones suggest they were poorer flyers than Ichthyornis.

65

SHOREBIRDS, GULLS, AUKS—Charadriiformes

A large order of 1 fossil and 13 living families. Principally waders, swimmers, divers, inhabiting the inland marshes and lakes and coastal waters, beaches, meadows of the world. Fossil record goes back some 75 million years to the Paleocene.

†CIMOLOPTERYX, Cimolopterygidae

4 species of primitive wading birds from the Upper Cretaceous of Wyoming, known from fragments of their wing bones.

JACANAS, Jacanidae

Distribution: 8 species, 7 living, 2 fossil to Miocene of Florida. 7 species Pan-tropical. 2 species Mexico to Argentina, 2 Africa, 1 Madagascar, 2 southern Asia to Australia. Marshy shores of rivers and lakes. Largely nonmigratory.

Characteristics: 6–20″. Wings short, rounded, often spurred; tail short, weak. Legs long; toes and claws very long. Usually a frontal shield. Ruddy to brown and black above, black, brown, or white below. Sexes similar, but female much larger than male.

Habits: Some gregarious. Run, swim, dive well, but flight weak, labored. Habitually walk on lily pads and other floating vegetation. Food, fish, mollusks, insects, some seeds of water plants. Eggs 4; incubated largely by male. Nest often partly afloat.

AFRICAN JACANA   12″
Actophilornis africanus
Africa south of the Sahara

United largely on anatomical characteristics of palate, syrinx, muscles, all have tufted oil gland, an aftershaft on body feathers. Most have 11 primaries, a few only 10. Colors not bright, generally black, white, brown. Plumage usually dense, often waterproof. Sexes usually alike. All except seedsnipe live on animal food.

GREATER PAINTED SNIPE   9½"
Rostratula benghalensis
Africa, Asia Minor to China, Japan,
Philippines, Australia

PAINTED SNIPES, Rostratulidae

Distribution: 2 species. 1 in s. South America, 1 in S. Africa, Madagascar, Asia Minor, India to Japan, Philippines, Malaya, Australia. In reedy marshes; slightly migratory.

Characteristics: 8–10". Wings short, rounded; flight weak; can swim short distances when they have to. Shortish bill, slightly decurved and swollen at tip. Greenish-brown above, whitish below. Female brighter and slightly larger than male.

Habits: Solitary or in small flocks. Rather retiring marsh birds; somewhat crepuscular. Feed on worms, mollusks, and other small swamp invertebrates—some vegetable food. Flight slow, rail-like, with dragging feet. Eggs 2–5. Apparently polyandrous. Incubation and rearing of young by male; incubation period 19 days.

DOUBLE-STRIPED THICK-KNEE 20"
Burhinus bistriatus
Hispaniola, southern Mexico
to northern Brazil

THICK-KNEES AND STONE CURLEWS, Burhinidae

Distribution: 9 species, temperate and tropical Eurasia, Africa, Malaya, Australia, Central and n. South America. In stony or sandy open country bordering rivers, lakes, and on grassy plains, sandy deserts. Northern species migratory; those of more tropical climes wander during the nonbreeding season but are not truly migratory.

Characteristics: 14–23". Wings moderately long, pointed; tail graduated. Eyes large; bill moderately short, stout. Legs fairly long; no hind toe; feet partly webbed. Their closest anatomical affinities are to the shorebirds, but in appearance and habits strongly resemble the bustards. Brownish birds streaked with gray and black; are difficult to see when crouched quietly on the ground. Sexes alike.

Habits: Nocturnal running birds; somewhat gregarious; fast runners; strong fliers. Crouch still on ground all day. Food insects, worms, snails, small animals. Nest on ground; eggs 2. Incubation largely by female; both care for precocial downy young.

COURSERS AND PRATINCOLES, Glareolidae

Distribution: 16 species, s. Eurasia, Africa, Australia; in sandy wastes, stony plains, grasslands, usually near water. Wander erratically when not breeding.

Characteristics: 6–12". Coursers, long legs; 3 toes; square tails; longish thin bill. Pratincoles, shorter legs; 4 toes; forked tails; short bills; wide gape. Plain dull brown or olivaceous birds with a few bold markings on head and neck. Sexes similar.

Habits: Gregarious birds. Pratincoles catch insects on the wing; fly like swallows. Coursers run swiftly, fly seldom but direct, fast. Also insectivorous. Eggs 2–3 in ground nest; incubation by female alone or by both sexes. Young precocial.

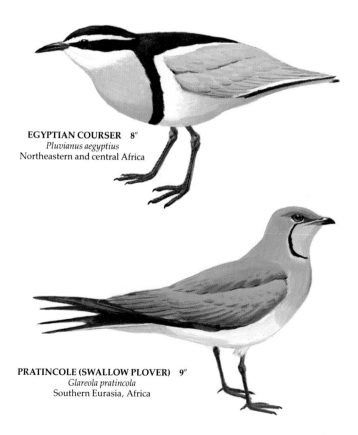

EGYPTIAN COURSER   8"
Pluvianus aegyptius
Northeastern and central Africa

PRATINCOLE (SWALLOW PLOVER)   9"
Glareola pratincola
Southern Eurasia, Africa

PLOVERS, LAPWINGS, Charadriidae

Distribution: 68 species, 63 living, 16 as fossil, to Oligocene of Colorado. Worldwide except Antarctica; in open, bare areas, coasts, plains, fields of short grass. Most species migratory.

Characteristics: 6–16″. Wading birds with short, rather stout bills usually swollen at tip; short, thick necks; long wings; short to medium tail; hind toe usually absent or vestigial. Adults usually bodly patterned in gray, brown, black, white. Sexes alike or very similar.

Habits: Rather gregarious. Run swiftly, gracefully, and stop abruptly. Food, animal matter in variety, some vegetable. Rarely wade when feeding. Calls melodious whistles, no true song. Eggs usually 4, spotted, conical; in ground nest, with incubation and care of young by both sexes or either predominant.

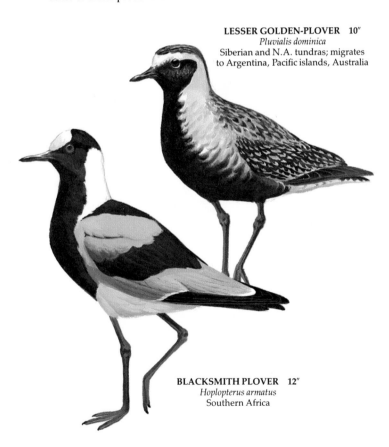

LESSER GOLDEN-PLOVER   10″
Pluvialis dominica
Siberian and N.A. tundras; migrates
to Argentina, Pacific islands, Australia

BLACKSMITH PLOVER   12″
Hoplopterus armatus
Southern Africa

EURASIAN OYSTERCATCHER 17″
Haematopus ostralegus
Eurasia

OYSTERCATCHERS, Haematopodidae

Distribution: 8 species, 6 living, 5 as fossil, to Miocene of Nebraska. Seen on practically all sea coasts of the world; a few on inland rivers; Iceland and Aleutians to Cape Horn, Cape of Good Hope, Tasmania. Some migratory.

Characteristics: 15–20″. Large, plover-like birds, with long, orange-red, blunt, knifelike bill. Exhibit two major color patterns. Plumage either all black or strongly pied, dark above, white below. Sexes alike. Toes 3.

Habits: Noisy, wary, usually gregarious birds of open sandy or rocky coasts. Call note is a loud, shrill, far-carrying repeated whistle. Flight strong, direct. Food mostly mollusks, sandworms, crustaceans. Nest on open beaches. Eggs 2–4; incubation and natal care by both sexes. The young remain with parents about 5 weeks.

71

SANDPIPERS AND ALLIES, Scolopacidae, Scolopacinae

Distribution: 110 species, 82 living, 69 as fossil, to Upper Cretaceous of New Jersey. Worldwide except Antarctica. Mostly in open areas, coastal beaches and marshes; a few in swamps, woodlands, fields, usually near water. Most species migratory.

Characteristics: 5–25″. Wading birds with long, slender bills, straight or downcurved, or broadened at end in one species; longish necks; hind toe usually present. Adults usually cryptically colored in grays, browns, white, often barred and spotted, seldom with bold contrasting colors. Sexes alike or very similar.

Habits: Quite gregarious, often in large flocks. Fast fliers. Most are waders, and probe in mud or sand for food. Voice highly varied; whistles, trills, harsh calls and alarm notes. Nest usually on ground; eggs 2–4. Incubation and natal care by either or both sexes.

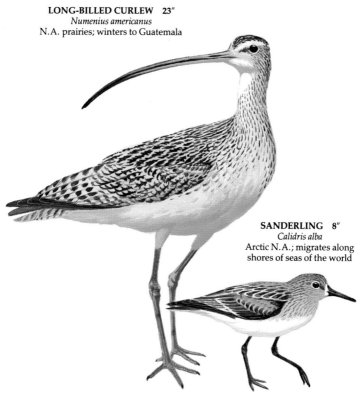

LONG-BILLED CURLEW   23″
Numenius americanus
N.A. prairies; winters to Guatemala

SANDERLING   8″
Calidris alba
Arctic N.A.; migrates along shores of seas of the world

MARBLED GODWIT   18″
Limosa fedoa
N.A. plains; winters to
costal Mexico, Peru, and Trinidad

SPOONBILL SANDPIPER   6″
Eurynorhynchus pygmeus
Coastal northeastern Siberia;
winters to
southeastern China, Assam, Burma

WILSON'S PHALAROPE   10"
Phalaropus tricolor
N.A. prairies; winters to Argentine pampas

PHALAROPES, Scolopacidae, Phalaropodinae

Distribution: 3 species. Northern parts of Northern Hemisphere. Breed near fresh pools in tundra; winter largely at sea in northern temperate and tropical latitudes. Migratory.

Characteristics: 7–10". Small "sea snipe" with long, pointed wings; long, thin, straight bill. Toes with individual lobate webs. Most aquatic members of shorebird complex; can swim as well as they can wade or walk. Gray and white in winter; in summer patterned with reds and browns. Females larger and brighter than males; the roles of the sexes are strongly reversed.

Habits: Only oceanic shore birds. Gregarious, in small flocks; are quite tame and unafraid. Spin around in water when feeding on crustacea, insects. Courtship by female. Lay 4 eggs in ground nest in the open tundra, always near water. Incubation and care of young by male alone.

STILTS AND AVOCETS, Recurvirostridae

Distribution: 7 species, temperate and tropical regions of most of the world; in open marshes or wet grasslands near fresh, brackish, or salt water. Northern populations migratory.

Characteristics: 12–20". Extremely long-legged wading birds; front toes partly webbed, hind toe vestigial or absent. Wings long, pointed; tail short, square. Bill straight, upturned, or decurved. Largely white with varying amounts of black above (1 species all gray). Sexes alike.

Habits: Gregarious, strong-flying birds of open wetlands; wade in shallows; swim readily. Loud, harsh voices. Stilts probe mud; avocets sweep water with bill. Eggs usually 4, in ground nest. Incubation and rearing by both parents.

BLACK-NECKED STILT   15"
Himantopus mexicanus
Central and southern N.A. to northern South America

AMERICAN AVOCET   18"
Recurvirostra americana
N.A. prairies; winters to
Mexico and Guatemala

SEEDSNIPES, Thinocoridae

Distribution: 4 species, western South America from Ecuador southward in open barren highlands or sparsely vegetated fields. Some species migratory.

Characteristics: 6–11". Plump, short-legged little birds with long, pointed wings and short, sparrow-like bills. Flap over nostrils. Hind toe present. Gray-brown above with buff markings; paler below with throat and breast markings. Sexes alike.

Habits: Gregarious terrestrial birds that run rapidly, crouch to hide on ground, flush suddenly into hurried, zigzag, snipe-like flight with sharp, scraping cries. Food largely seeds, grasses, some insects. Nesting poorly known.

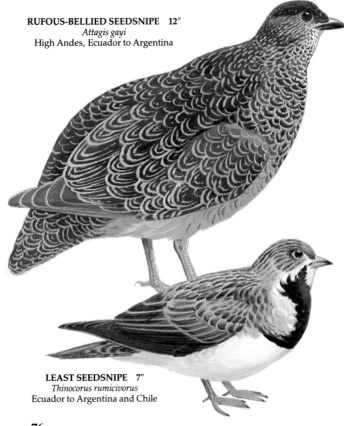

RUFOUS-BELLIED SEEDSNIPE   12"
Attagis gayi
High Andes, Ecuador to Argentina

LEAST SEEDSNIPE   7"
Thinocorus rumicivorus
Ecuador to Argentina and Chile

SHEATHBILLS, Chionididae

Distribution: 2 species. Antarctic and subantarctic islands and coasts from Cape Horn and Palmer Peninsula e. to Heard and Kerguellen Islands. Rocky coasts. Wander locally.

Characteristics: 15″. Pure white, pigeon-like birds with short, stout bills and legs; saddle-shaped horny sheath over upper bill at base. Face and bill with fleshy wattles. Toes slightly webbed; hind toe present. Rudimentary spur on wing. Sexes alike. Structurally, the sheathbills are a connecting link between the shorebirds and the gulls; perhaps fairly direct descendents of an ancient common ancestor from which both groups diverged.

Habits: Gregarious, social, tame, quarrelsome birds. Largely terrestrial, but make long overwater flights. Swim well but seldom. Omnivorous scavengers in bird and seal colonies; especially flock around calving sea elephants to gorge themselves on afterbirths and droppings. Also eat wide variety of animal food (mollusks, crustaceans, etc.) and seaweed. Eggs 2–3; young precocial. Both sexes incubate.

SNOWY SHEATHBILL 16″
Chionis alba
Subantarctic coasts and islands

CRAB PLOVER, Dromadidae

Distribution: 1 species, coasts of Red Sea, Persian Gulf, and n. and w. Indian Ocean; on rocky and sandy seashores and shores of salt lakes. Migratory.

Characteristics: 15″. Are sociable birds, easily approached and not at all shy. Wings long, pointed; tail short; bill long, compressed, strong, heron-like. Legs long, front toes semipalmate, hind toe present. White with black mantle and flight feathers, and gray-blue legs. Sexes alike; male slightly larger.

Habits: Gregarious, conspicuous wading birds. They have a peculiar upright stance and fly strongly with neck and feet outstretched; run fast. Feed along coasts on crabs, mollusks. Crepuscular. Are usually found in flocks and nest colonially in burrows in sand banks. Lay 1 large, white egg. Precocial young hatch covered with gray down; can run soon after hatching.

CRAB PLOVER   15″
Dromas ardeola
Coasts of northeast Africa,
southwest Asia

LONG-TAILED JAEGER 22"
Stercorarius longicaudus
Circumpolar on arctic
coasts and islands;
winters to southern oceans

GREAT SKUA 23"
Catharacta skua
Iceland, Faroes, Shetlands; circumpolar
on subantarctic coasts and islands

SKUAS AND JAEGERS, Laridae, Stercorariinae

Distribution: 6 species, 5 living, 4 as fossil, to Pleistocene of Oregon. Breed in tundra and barren coasts and islands of Arctic and Antarctic; winter largely at sea and off coasts of all oceans except central Pacific.

Characteristics: 16–24". Jaegers' wings long, pointed; tail medium to long with elongated central feathers. Bill hooked, with cere for nostrils. Feet webbed; hallux small. Skuas dark brown; jaegers brown above with brown to white below (2 color phases). Sexes alike.

Habits: Somewhat gregarious; partly pelagic predators. Flight fast and strong. Food mammals, eggs and young of other birds; harass terns, gulls into dropping fish. Simple nest on ground; eggs 2, incubated by both sexes. Precocious downy young partly nidicolous.

79

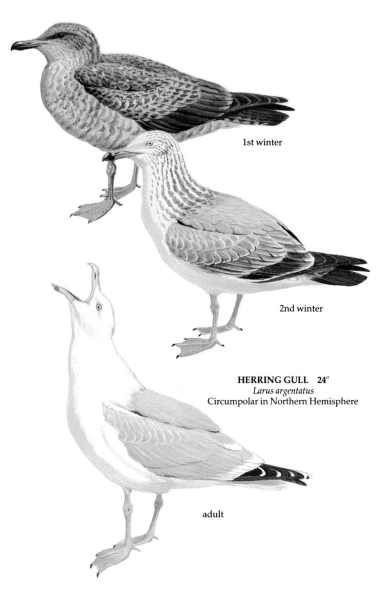

1st winter

2nd winter

HERRING GULL   24″
Larus argentatus
Circumpolar in Northern Hemisphere

adult

80

GULLS AND TERNS, Laridae, Larinae, Sterninae

Distribution: 96 species, 82 living (43 gulls, 39 terns), 42 fossil, to Eocene of England. Worldwide except continental Antarctica. Typically coastal marine; many species on inland lakes, rivers, ponds, marshes. Most species migratory, some highly so.

Characteristics: 8–32". Water birds with long, pointed wings; short to medium legs; webbed feet; short hallux. Gulls usually larger, with stout hooked bill and squarish tail. Terns smaller, with more slender bodies, straight pointed bill, forked tail. Typically white birds with gray backs or black wingtips, dark heads or crests; some all black or all brown. Sexes alike.

Habits: Gregarious; strong fliers; often noisy. Gulls omnivorous, often scavenge; soar frequently; swim well; pick up food from surface and from land. Terns usually dive for minnows; do not soar; swim poorly. All nest colonially; nest usually on ground, poorly built; eggs 1–4; incubation and natal care by both sexes.

COMMON TERN 15"
Sterna hirundo
Temperate Northern Hemisphere

BROWN NODDY 15"
Anous stolidus
Tropical seas of the world

BLACK SKIMMER 20″
Rynchops niger
Western Hemisphere coasts
from Massachusetts
and Mexico to Straits of Magellan

SKIMMERS, Laridae, Rynchopinae

Distribution: 3 species. Eastern U.S. s. to Argentina, Chile; tropical Africa; India to Southeast Asia; on sheltered sandy seacoasts and large rivers. Partly migratory.

Characteristics: 15–20″. Long, knifelike bill with lower mandible longer than upper. Wings long, pointed; webbed feet small; short forked tail. Black or brown above, white below; bill and feet black or yellow. Sexes alike.

Habits: Gregarious water birds that feed by flying over water with lower bill cutting surface. Wingbeat shallow, mostly above body. Crepuscular. Voice a doglike yelp. Eggs 2–5 in scrape in sand. Incubation by female; both sexes feed downy nidifugous young.

AUKS, MURRES, PUFFINS, Alcidae

Distribution: 39 species, 21 living, 1 recently extinct, 35 fossil, to Eocene of Utah. Northern parts of Northern Hemisphere; in cold salt waters, mostly off rocky coasts. Partly migratory.

Characteristics: 6½–19". Small to medium-sized sea birds with chunky bodies, short necks, small pointed wings, short legs set far back, 3 front toes webbed, no hind toe. Bills highly variable. Mostly black above, white below; some all dark. Sexes alike.

Habits: Gregarious; fly strongly with rapid even wingbeat when airborne. Fine swimmers and divers; use wings under water. Food, fish and other marine animals. Nest colonially, on rocky cliffs, ledges, crevices; some in burrows. Eggs 1–2; incubated by female or both parents. Both feed precocial but nidicolous young.

COMMON MURRE 17"
Uria aalge
N. Atlantic, Pacific, and Arctic coasts

ATLANTIC PUFFIN 12"
Fratercula arctica
North Atlantic coasts

RAZORBILL 16"
Alca torda
Coasts of n. North Atlantic

PIGEONS—Columbiformes

An order of 2 living families and 1 recently extinct of distinctive land birds that show no close ties to any other order. They occur the world around except in the polar regions. Most are plump-bodied birds with short bills,

PALLAS'S SANDGROUSE 15″
Syrrhaptes paradoxus
Central Siberian plains

SANDGROUSE, Pteroclididae

Distribution: 19 species, 16 living, 5 fossil, to Eocene of France. Central and southern Eurasia, Africa, Madagascar, in open sandy or rocky deserts and plains with thin cover. Some migrate eruptively and sporadically.

Characteristics: 9–16″. Stout-bodied, pigeon-like birds with very short, feathered legs and feet, and long, pointed wings and tail. Cryptically colored in grays, browns, mottled black, white, orange. Females smaller and more heavily marked. Vocabularies include whistles, clucking, and croaking noises; twitter continually on long flights.

Habits: Gregarious; shy ground birds that walk with mincing steps, fly fast and straight with short quick wingstrokes. Eat seeds, berries, insects. In dry regions fly long distances to water daily. Eggs 2–3 in a ground scrape with little lining. Incubation and natal care by both sexes; female incubates by day, the male by night.

culmen downcurved, and dense plumage that is easily detached. Down in adults is absent or scarce and found on apteria only. Legs usually short; feet not webbed; toes short.

Food mainly vegetable matter, fruits, grains, herbage. Feed young by regurgitation from large crop.

DODOS, SOLITAIRES, Raphidae

Distribution: 3 species, Mascarene Islands; in forested interiors. Dodo extinct since 1680; solitaires since 1800.

Characteristics: 25–50 lbs. Heavy-bodied birds with ridiculous short wings; heavy hooked beaks; short, stout legs. Tail of loose, curly feathers. Grayish-brown to white; males larger; females more brightly colored.

Habits: Large, forest-living, flightless ground birds. Ate fruits, seeds, leaves, berries. Laid a single egg on ground. Incubation by both sexes. Exterminated by introduced pigs and monkeys.

DODO 45″
Raphus cucullatus
Mauritius Island

PIGEONS, DOVES, Columbidae

Distribution: 298 species, 284 living, 5 lately extinct, 38 fossil, to Miocene of France. Worldwide in temperate and tropical regions. Mostly arboreal forest dwellers; some terrestrial in open lands. Many species migratory, especially northern ones.

Characteristics: 6–33". Compact, full-breasted birds with rather short necks and small heads. Bill relatively small and slender, constricted in middle, and with a fleshy cere at base. Colors widely varied. Sexes alike or nearly so.

Habits: Gregarious or solitary. Most are strong, fast fliers. Eat seeds, fruit, some insects, worms. Eggs 1–3; usually in a frail platform nest; incubated by both parents. Young fed "pigeons's milk" from parent's crop.

WOOD PIGEON   16"
Columba palumbus
Europe, western Asia

THICK-BILLED GREEN PIGEON   10"
Treron curvirostris
Southeast Asia and through Malaysia

ELEGANT IMPERIAL PIGEON 17″
Ducula concinna
Eastern Indonesian islands

VICTORIA CROWNED PIGEON 28″
Goura victoria
Northern New Guinea

87

PARROTS AND RELATIVES—Psittaciformes

PARROTS AND RELATIVES, Psittacidae

Distribution: 339 species, 317 living, 15 lately extinct, 26 fossil, to Miocene of France. The world around in tropics and subtropics; Central and South America, Africa, s. Asia, Malaya, Madagascar, Australia, New Zealand. Almost all arboreal, most nonmigratory.

Characteristics: 3–40″. Large-headed, short-necked birds with powerful hooked beak with a cere (sometimes feathered). Legs short; feet strong; 2 toes in front, 2 behind. Tongue thick, fleshy, sometimes fringed. Lores often bare. Plumage sparse, hard, often glossy, usually gaudy–greens, reds, yellows. Sexes usually alike.

Habits: Usually gregarious; most are forest inhabitants. Fly strongly but seldom far. Climb with bill. Voices raucous, nonimitative in wild. Food largely fruit, grains, nuts, nectar. Nest usually in unlined hollows in trees, rocks, banks, termite nests. Eggs 1–12, white; incubated by both sexes. Young fed by regurgitation.

TURQUOISE-FRONTED PARROT   18″
Amazona aestiva
Brazil and Bolivia to n. Argentina

HYACINTH MACAW   34″
Anodorhynchus hyacinthinus
Brazil and Bolivia
to northern Argentina

BUDGERIGAR   7"
Melopsittacus undulatus
Australia

GREATER BLACK COCKATOO   32"
Probosciger aterrimus
New Guinea, northern Australia

BLACK-CAPPED LORY   11"
Domicella domicella
Ceram and Amboina islands

89

CUCKOOS AND ALLIES—Cuculiformes

An order of 2 families of land birds most nearly related to the parrots. Two toes in front, 2 behind, but 8–10 tail feathers instead of 12–14. Upper bill not movable, never hooked, and no cere. Found the world around in temperate and tropical regions.

TOURACOS, Musophagidae

Distribution: 21 species, 18 living, 3 fossil, to Eocene of France. Africa south of Sahara; in dense jungle, forest edges. Local movement but no migration.

Characteristics: 15–29″. Wings short, rounded; bill short, stout; neck longish; head small and usually crested; tail long. Soft plumage in solid green, blue, brown, or gray, marked with red or white. Sexes alike.

Habits: Arboreal birds usually in pairs or family groups. Flight weak and dipping. Climb and run, squirrel-fashion, through foliage. Noisy but not conspicuous. Eat fruit, seeds, buds, insects, larvae. Eggs 2–3, white. Downy young nidicolous. Incubation and natal care by both sexes.

RED-CRESTED TOURACO 16″
Turacus erythrolophus
Angola through Zaire

GREATER ROADRUNNER 23″
Geococcyx californianus
Southwestern U.S. and Mexico

COMMON CUCKOO 13″
Cuculus canorus
Eurasia, Africa

SMOOTH-BILLED ANI 13″
Crotophaga ani
West Indies, Mexico to Argentina

CUCKOOS, ANIS, ROADRUNNERS, COUCALS, Cuculidae

Distribution: 130 species, 125 living, 1 lately extinct, 15 fossil, to Eocene of Wyoming. Cosmopolitan in tropic and temperate zones, except Oceania and high continental latitudes. Live in forests or open brush country. Northern species migratory.

Characteristics: 6–30″. Slim-bodied, long-tailed birds with rather stout, decurved bills (compressed in anis); short legs. Loose plumage dull colored in grays, browns, sometimes barred (black in anis), metallic green and yellow in some. Sexes usually alike.

Habits: Mostly arboreal birds, a few terrestrial. Run well along tree branches and on ground. Flight weak and slow to strong and fast. Many Old World and 1 New World species parasitic in nesting. Others vary widely in type of nest. Eggs 2–6, incubated by both sexes. Young naked, nidicolous.

OWLS—Strigiformes

An order of 1 fossil and 2 living families found the world around except in Antarctica and Oceania. Soft-feathered birds. Their large eyes are directed forward and set on a facial disk. Feet are stout and strong with long, sharp claws.

†PROTOSTRIX, Protostrigidae
5 fossil species to Eocene of Wyoming.

BARN OWLS, Tytonidae

Distribution: 21 species, 10 living, 12 fossil, to Miocene of France. Cosmopolitan; absent from polar regions, New Zealand, and most oceanic islands. Live in forests and open, cultivated lands. Largely nonmigratory.

Characteristics: 13–21". Facial disk heart-shaped; legs longer than tail; tail but not primaries emarginate. Middle claw with comb. Tarsus feathered; toes bare. Golden-brown above, white below, marked with gray, white, black. Sexes similar; female often larger.

Habits: Usually solitary, nocturnal, seldom seen by daylight. Flight buoyant, noiseless. Food small mammals, some birds, reptiles, amphibians, insects. Swallow food whole and regurgitate pellets. Make no nest. Lay 4-7 eggs in hollow tree, building, or on ground. Incubation by female; care of nidicolous young by both parents.

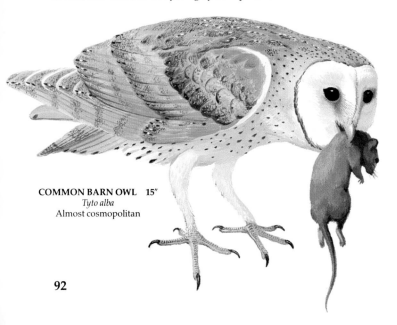

COMMON BARN OWL   15"
Tyto alba
Almost cosmopolitan

Quiet-flying, largely nocturnal birds of prey. Food almost entirely higher vertebrates. Regurgitate pellets of bones, fur, feathers. Have varied weird calls; also snap bill audibly. Lay spherical white eggs in holes in trees, burrows, buildings, nests of other birds.

EAGLE OWL   25″
Bubo bubo
Eurasia

TYPICAL OWLS, Strigidae

Distribution: 153 species; 121 living, 2 lately extinct, 55 fossil, to Oligocene of France. Worldwide except Antarctica and some oceanic islands. In almost all types of habitat. Most species sedentary.

Characteristics: 5½–30″. Facial disk rounded. Legs shorter than tail. Earlike tufts in many species. Flank feathers elongate; tarsus, toes in some species feathered. Colored mottled grays to red browns and white. Sexes alike; female often larger.

Habits: Mostly nocturnal, a few diurnal. Flight quiet in nocturnal species, not in diurnal. Food, varied animal matter. Voice varied. Nest in holes and old nests of other birds. Eggs 1–7, white, rounded; incubated by female or by both; care of downy, nidicolous young by both.

GOATSUCKERS AND ALLIES—
Caprimugiformes

An order of 5 families of nocturnal or crepuscular birds found throughout the world south of latitude 60° N., except Antarctica, in varied habitats.

Soft-feathered birds with long, pointed wings, short,

OILBIRD 18″
Steatornis caripensis
Trinidad and northern South America

OILBIRD, Steatornithidae

Distribution: 1 species. Ecuador and Peru east to French Guiana and Trinidad, in semiopen country. Nonmigratory.

Characteristics: 18″. Wings and tail long; legs and feet small, weak, unscaled. Toes long; claws sharp. Bill short, strong, downcurved, hooked; long rictal bristles. Chestnut-brown spotted with white, barred with black. Sexes alike.

Habits: Gregarious. Flight strong, silent. Hover to feed, mainly on palm nuts. Forage widely from seaside or mountain cave where they roost by day and also nest. Weird cries; echo-ranging clicking. Eggs 2–4, white; incubated by both sexes.

weak legs and feet, very small bill, but wide, gaping mouth. Colored browns or grays mottled with black or darker browns and grays. Sexes similar.

Mostly solitary (a few gregarious); flight strong, erratic, batlike. Food largely insects caught on the wing. Eyes reflect light at night. Nest on ground, in trees, in caves. Eggs 1–5, usually 1–2.

FROGMOUTHS, Podargidae

Distribution: 12 species, s.e. Asia, East Indies, Australia, Philippines, Solomons; in lowland forests, brushlands. Partly migratory.

Characteristics: 9–12″. Wings moderate, rounded; tail long, pointed. Bill broad, heavy, flat, triangular, horny. Legs short, feet small, weak; long middle toe. Cryptic browns, grays: often two color phases. Sexes similar.

Habits: Solitary or in pairs. Rather weak fliers that live on creeping insects and small animals caught on ground or branches. Nest in trees, a platform or pad of sticks, feathers, lichens. Eggs 1–2; incubated by both sexes. Downy young nidicolous.

TAWNY FROGMOUTH 19″
Podargus strigoides
Australia and Tasmania

POTOOS, Nyctibiidae

Distribution: 5 species, s. Mexico and West Indies to Paraguay, n. Argentina. In open forested country. Nonmigratory.

Characteristics: 14–19″. Wings and tail long, pointed; small bill toothed. No rictal bristles; no comb on middle claw. Cryptically colored grays, browns. Sexes alike.

Habits: Solitary, nocturnal. Perch upright on stubs or branches. Dash out from perch to catch insects on wing, like flycatchers. Egg 1, usually atop broken tree stub. Downy, nidicolous young.

OWLET FROGMOUTHS, Aegothelidae

Distribution: 9 species, 8 living, 1 fossil from New Zealand Quaternary. Australia, New Guinea, New Caledonia. In open forest, dense brushlands. Nonmigratory.

Characteristics: 6–12″. Wings long, rounded; tail long, pointed. Feet small, weak; toes and claws long, slender; no comb on middle toe. Brownish-gray feathers mottled with brown and black. Sexes are similar.

Habits: Solitary; nocturnal. Usually stay in hollow tree by day and feed at night, hawking insects both in air and on ground. Flight straight, deliberate. Nest in hollow tree; eggs 3–5. Downy young nidicolous.

COMMON POTOO 14″
Nyctibius griseus
Mexico to Argentina

GRAY OWLET FROGMOUTH 6″
Aegotheles albertisi
New Guinea

COMMON NIGHTHAWK 9"
Chordeiles minor
Temperate North America

RED-NECKED NIGHTJAR 12"
Caprimulgus ruficollis
Spain, northern Africa

NIGHTJARS, Caprimulgidae

Distribution: 67 species. 67 living, 8 fossil to Pleistocene of Brazil. Cosmopolitan, s. of Arctic Circle and n. of latitude 40° S. Absent from New Zealand and most oceanic islands. Varied habitats; some species migratory.

Characteristics: 7–12" (extremely long wing and tail feathers in 2 species). Wings long, pointed; tail medium to long. Feet small, weak; comb on middle claw. Eyes large. Colored cryptically in grays, browns; feathers barred, mottled. Sexes similar but usually unlike.

Habits: Usually solitary; some migrate in loose flocks. Nocturnal or crepuscular. Food insects caught in flight. Flight strong. Perch on branches lengthwise. Eggs 1–2, on bare or littered ground. Incubation and natal care by both sexes. At least one species hibernates.

SWIFTS AND HUMMINGBIRDS—Apodiformes

An order of 1 fossil and 3 living families of strong-winged, weak-footed birds found throughout the world except in the polar regions, New Zealand, and oceanic islands. All are strong fliers that feed on the wing; lay small clutches of white eggs; young hatch naked and blind and require long fledging period.

†AEGIALORNIS, Aegialornithidae

2 fossil species from the Upper Eocene or Lower Oligocene of France.

CRESTED SWIFTS, Hemiprocnidae

Distribution: 3 species, s.e. Asia, East Indies, Philippines e. to Solomons. Forest edges, clearings, open wooded hillsides. Nonmigratory.

Characteristics: 6½–13". Head crested; tail long, forked. Neck short; eyes large. Hind toe not reversible. Plumage soft; blue-grays to browns with metallic gloss. Sexes unlike.

Habits: Gregarious. Flight powerful, fast, wheeling, not so sustained as in swifts. Perch and nest on high branches. Roost huddled together. Cement single egg to extremely small platform nest. Incubation and natal care by both sexes.

INDIAN CRESTED SWIFT   8-9"
Hemiprocne longipennis
India to Southeast Asia and Sulawesi

Whether hummingbirds are correctly placed here is a matter of conjecture. That they share a common ancestor with swifts is not certain. They show considerable differences in their bone development and in their feeding and nesting habits.

SWIFTS, Apodidae

Distribution: 71 species, 66 living, 10 fossil to Oligocene of France. Cosmopolitan except high latitudes, oceanic islands, New Zealand. Many migratory.

Characteristics: 3½–10″. Wings long, narrow, pointed. Feet tiny; hind toe reversible in some; claws strongly curved. Tail variable, often spiny. Neck short; body streamlined. Bill small; gape wide. Dusky browns, blacks, some with white or pale throat, rump, flanks. Sexes alike.

Habits: Usually gregarious; among most aerial of all birds. Live on insects caught in flight. Seldom alight on ground or branches; rest on sides of cliffs, caves, hollow trees. Glue nest of twigs together with sticky saliva. Both sexes incubate and rear young.

CHIMNEY SWIFT 5″
Chaetura pelagica
Temperate central and eastern N. America;
winters to northern South America

**EDIBLE-NEST
SWIFTLET 5″**
Collocalia inexpectata
India to Southeast Asia,
Philippines, East Indies

HUMMINGBIRDS, Trochilidae

Distribution: 319 species, temperate and tropical Americas in forests, savannas, brushlands, desert. Some migratory.

Characteristics: 2½–6½". Wings long, narrow; tail variable; legs short; feet tiny, weak; bill slender, pointed, straight or curved; sternum and flying muscles large. Color highly varied, mainly browns, greens, blacks, with iridescent patches of metallic red, gold, purple. Sexes usually unlike.

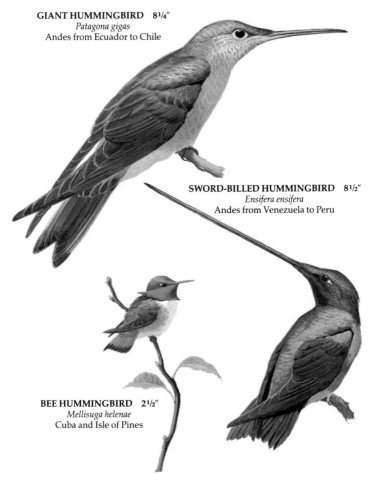

GIANT HUMMINGBIRD 8¼"
Patagona gigas
Andes from Ecuador to Chile

SWORD-BILLED HUMMINGBIRD 8½"
Ensifera ensifera
Andes from Venezuela to Peru

BEE HUMMINGBIRD 2½"
Mellisuga helenae
Cuba and Isle of Pines

WHITE-TIPPED SICKLEBILL 5″
Eutoxeres aquila
Costa Rica to Ecuador

BLUE-THROATED SYLPH 7½″
Aglaiocercus kingi
Andes from Venezuela to Peru, Bolivia

WHITE-CRESTED COQUETTE 3″
Lophornis adorabilis
Costa Rica

Habits: Solitary. Flight powerful, agile, with very fast wingbeats. Perch readily but do not walk or climb. Food flower nectar, small insects. Pugnacious. Voices weak. Eggs usually 2, in deep cup nest of plant fibers, spider webs, lichens. Male takes little or no part in nesting duties.

101

COLIES OR MOUSEBIRDS—Coliiformes

Show no close affinities to any other bird groups.

COLIES, Coliidae

Distribution: 9 species, 6 living, 3 fossil from Miocene of France. Warm parts of Africa south of Sahara, in somewhat open country, brushlands, forest edges. Nonmigratory.

Characteristics: 11½–14″. Wings short, rounded; tail long, pointed. Legs short; feet stout; toes and claws long; outer toe reversible. Soft-plumaged, crested, gray-brown birds variably marked with black and white. Feet and bill usually red. Sexes alike.

Habits: Gregarious; roost in compact groups usually touching each other; often sleep head downward. Flight fast and straight but not sustained. Eat fruit, seeds, shoots, leaves; damage crops, gardens. Creep through trees climbing with bill. Eggs 2–4 in shallow nest in tree or shrub. Incubation and natal care by both sexes.

WHITE-HEADED MOUSEBIRD 13″
Colius leucocephalus
Tropical eastern Africa

**BLUE-CROWNED
TROGON** 9½"
Trogon curucui
Colombia to northern Argentina

TROGONS—Trogoniformes

Bright-colored tropical birds with no close relatives.

TROGONS, Trogonidae

Distribution: 39 species, 35 living, 6 fossil to Oligocene of France. Pantropical. Arizona, West Indies to n. Argentina; e. and s. Africa; India, Malaya, Philippines. Principally in dense jungle forest.

Characteristics: 9–13½". Wings short, semi-round; tail long, broad, truncate. Legs and feet small, weak; tarsus feathered; 1st and 2nd toes backward. Bill short, wide, serrate in New World species. Skin very tender; plumage very soft; fluffy, bright greens, blacks, reds, yellows, blues, often metallic. Sexes usually unlike.

Habits: Solitary arboreal birds that sit quietly on high branches in dark forests and utter simple, melancholy calls. Old World forms live principally on insects; American species also eat fruit. Nest in hollow tree or in termite nest. Eggs 2–4, rounded, white to greenish-blue, unmarked. Young hatch naked; nidicolous. Both sexes incubate and rear young.

KINGFISHERS AND ALLIES—Coraciiformes

An order of 10 families of usually conspicuous birds found throughout the world in temperate and tropical zones, usually in forested areas. Most are brightly colored, and have large, prominent bills.

TODIES, Todidae

Distribution: 5 species, limited to Greater Antilles of West Indies; in wooded or brushy hillsides and ravines, often near streams. Nonmigratory.

Characteristics: 3¹/₂–4¹/₂". Wings short, rounded; legs and feet slender, weak; bill long, straight, flattened, dull red. Tiny birds with green backs, red throats, lighter underparts washed with yellow or pink. Sexes alike.

Habits: Tame, unsuspicious, arboreal birds usually found in pairs. Voices harsh, chattering, chipping. Also clatter bills audibly. Wings make audible whir in flight. Feed like flycatchers, darting out from a branch and returning at once with their insect prey. Nest in unlined, deep burrow in bank. Both sexes incubate and feed young.

CUBAN TODY   4"
Todus multicolor
Cuba

INDIAN THREE-TOED KINGFISHER   5"
Ceyx erithacus
India to the Philippines

Many are somewhat gregarious; most are noisy. All are carnivorous, eat fish, small animals, insects. A few also eat fruit and berries. All are hole-nesters; usually lay 3–10 eggs, white or slightly tinted, seldom marked. Young usually hatch naked, always blind, nidicolous.

KINGFISHERS, Alcedinidae

Distribution: 89 species, 86 living, 1 recently extinct, 7 fossil to Oligocene of Switzerland. Worldwide except polar regions and some oceanic islands; in forested or savanna country, usually near water. Higher latitude species migratory.

Characteristics: 4–18″. Wings short, rounded; tail short to very long. Legs small, weak. Body often stout, compact; neck short; head quite large. Bill long, heavy, pointed. Highly varied, but usually bright-colored birds, often crested. Sexes alike and unlike.

Habits: Solitary birds that hover over water to dive on fish, or sit upright and still on an exposed perch to watch for prey, dashing out for insects in air or critters on ground. Nest in unlined hole in bank, tree, or termitaria. Both sexes incubate and care for young.

BLUE-BREASTED KINGFISHER   10″
Halcyon malimbicus
Southwestern Africa

KOOKABURRA   17″
Dacelo gigas
Eastern and southern Australia

RIVER KINGFISHER   6½″
Alcedo atthis
Eurasia, Africa, Oceania

MOTMOTS, Momotidae

Distribution: 8 species. Mexico south to n. Argentina and Paraguay. Tobago, Trinidad islands. In heavy forests, usually near streams. Nonmigratory.

Characteristics: 6–20″. Wings short, rounded; tail long, often racket-tipped. Bill strong, downcurved, often serrate. Legs short. Loose-webbed plumage of greens, blues, browns. Often a breast spot. Sexes closely similar.

Habits: Neither shy nor gregarious; usually solitary or in pairs. Sit motionless for long periods on low branch. Dash out to catch insects; also eat reptiles, some fruit. Wag tail stiffly, irregularly from side to side. Nest in holes in trees, banks. Incubation by both sexes. Young nidicolous.

BLUE-CROWNED MOTMOT 16″
Momotus momota
Mexico to Argentina

TODY MOTMOT 7″
Hylomanes momotula
Mexico to Colombia

BLUE-CHEEKED BEE-EATER 11″
Merops superciliosus
Western Asia, Africa, Madagascar

BLUE-HEADED BEE-EATER 11″
Melittophagus mulleri
Central Africa

BEE-EATER, Meropidae

Distribution: 24 species. Old World temperate and tropic zones; s. Europe, s. China, East Indies to Solomons, Africa, Australia. In forested or open country. Temperate zone breeders migratory; tropic forms move locally following food.

Characteristics: 6–14″. Wings large, pointed; tail long, usually with two central feathers elongated. Bill slender, ridged, slightly downcurved, pointed. Feet small, weak. Brilliantly colored, mainly greens with bold patches of red, blue, yellow, brown. Sexes similar.

Habits: Usually gregarious; arboreal birds that perch on exposed branches, wires, roofs. Hawk insects or catch them in short sallies. Flight easy, graceful, strong, sometimes erratic. Voice unmelodious. Nest in ground burrow. Incubation and natal care by both sexes.

ROLLERS, Coraciidae

Distribution: 12 species, 11 living, 4 fossil to Oligocene of France. Africa s. of Sahara, s. Eurasia to Australia, Solomons; in forests, brushlands, farmlands, trees about villages. Some species migratory.

Characteristics: 10–16″. Wings long, pointed; tail usually short, square, or forked. Bill strong, broad; neck short; legs short, weak. Heavy, jay-like, gaudy birds with blues, greens predominating. Sexes alike or nearly so.

Habits: Usually solitary arboreal birds. Perch on exposed branches; dart out for flying insects and for small vertebrates on ground. Noisy, pugnacious, attack other birds. Both sexes have spectacular courtship flight with rolling and turning. Nest in hollow trees, burrows, abandoned nests. Incubation and natal care by both sexes. Young hatch naked; nidicolous.

BLACK-BILLED (INDIAN) ROLLER   13″
Coracias benghalensis
Southeast Asia

DOLLAR BIRD;
BROAD-BILLED ROLLER   12″
Eurystomus orientalis
S. India to Japan, East Indies, northern Australia

LONG-TAILED GROUND-ROLLER 15"
Uratelornis chimaera
Madagascar

KIROMBO CUCKOO-ROLLER 12"
Leptosomus discolor
Madagascar

GROUND-ROLLERS, Brachypteraciidae

Distribution: 5 species. Madagascar; in heavy forests, brushlands. Nonmigratory.

Characteristics: 12–17". Shorter wings, longer legs than rollers, and longer pointed tails. More cryptically colored in yellows, greens, browns. Sexes similar.

Habits: Solitary, crepuscular, terrestrial birds. Rolling flight when excited. Hunt on ground. Nest in ground holes. Eat insects, small vertebrates.

CUCKOO-ROLLER, Leptosomatidae

Distribution: 1 species. Madagascar and Comoro Islands; forests, brushlands. Nonmigratory.

Characteristics: 18". Wings long, pointed; tail long, truncate. Legs short; toes long; 4th toe rotated to side. Powder downs present. Dark gray to brown with metallic reflection above, lighter below. Sexes unlike.

Habits: Somewhat gregarious; small flocks fly above forest. Feed in treetops on insects, lizards. Loud voices. Nesting little known.

HOOPOE, Upupidae

Distribution: 1 species. Central and southern Eurasia, Africa except Sahara, Madagascar. In forests, semiopen, and cultivated lands. Some populations migratory.

Characteristics: 12″. Wings broad, rounded; tail moderate, square. Bill long, thin, slightly downcurved. A strongly crested, pinkish-brown bird, barred black and white on tail and wings. Sexes similar; female smaller, duller.

Habits: Usually solitary or in pairs, or small flocks. Flight undulating and erratic. Loud voice, *hoop-hoop*. Feed on ground probing for ants, worms; hawk insects in flight. Perch, roost in trees. Nest in cavity in tree, wall, building. Male feeds female on nest. Nest filthy. Female has strong odor when nesting.

HOOPOE   11″
Upupa epops
Eurasia, Africa,
Madagascar

GREEN WOOD-HOOPOE   13″
Phoeniculus purpureus
Africa south of Sahara

WOOD-HOOPOES, Phoeniculidae

Distribution: 6 species. Africa s. of Sahara; in heavy forests, wooded grasslands. Local movements, but nonmigratory.

Characteristics: 9–17″. Wings rounded; tail long, graduated. Bill long, thin, strongly downcurved to almost straight. Legs short, partly feathered in some; claws long, curved. Plumage dark with blue to green metallic gloss. Sexes similar; female smaller, sometimes browner.

Habits: Solitary or in small groups. Arboreal; fly short distances from tree to tree. Run and climb on trunks and branches, often head down. Eat insects, small fruits. Shy, wary; nest in tree cavities. Incubation by female; care of young by both parents. Loud chattering noises.

110

HORNBILLS, Bucerotidae

Distribution: 46 species, 44 living, 3 fossil to Eocene of Germany. Africa s. of Sahara, s. Arabia to Southeast Asia, Malaysia, Philippines to Solomons. In heavy forests, brushlands. Nonmigratory.

Characteristics: 15–65″. Strong wings moderately long; tail long; legs short. Enormous bill surmounted by grotesque casque. Bill and bare facial skin often bright red or yellow. Coarse, loose-webbed plumage usually black or brown with bold markings. Sexes alike or similar; female smaller, duller.

Habits: Noisy, conspicuous birds, usually in pairs or small flocks. Flight strong but slow, labored, audible. Omnivorous, mostly eat insects, fruit, small animals. Nest in tree hollow; female walled in and fed by male until young are half fledged. Voices harsh.

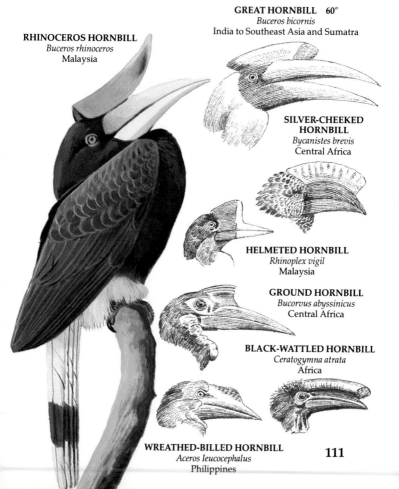

GREAT HORNBILL   60″
Buceros bicornis
India to Southeast Asia and Sumatra

RHINOCEROS HORNBILL
Buceros rhinoceros
Malaysia

SILVER-CHEEKED HORNBILL
Bycanistes brevis
Central Africa

HELMETED HORNBILL
Rhinoplex vigil
Malaysia

GROUND HORNBILL
Bucorvus abyssinicus
Central Africa

BLACK-WATTLED HORNBILL
Ceratogymna atrata
Africa

WREATHED-BILLED HORNBILL
Aceros leucocephalus
Philippines

111

WOODPECKERS AND ALLIES—Piciformes

An order of 6 families of arboreal birds found in the forested areas of the world except for Australia, New Zealand, Madagascar, and oceanic islands. They are distinguished mainly by their yoke-toed feet, usually 2 toes in front and 2 behind, occasionally only 1 behind, and by special leg-muscle formulas and other internal anatomical characteristics.

SPOTTED PUFFBIRD   7″
Bucco tamatia
Southern Venezuela to Brazil, Ecuador, Peru

PUFFBIRDS, Bucconidae

Distribution: 31 species, 30 living, 3 fossil to Eocene of Wyoming; in tropic forests from s. Mexico to s. Brazil and Paraguay. Nonmigratory.

Characteristics: 6–12″. Wings short, rounded; tail medium to long, square. Legs short. Head large; bill strong, flat, often hooked, with conspicuous rictal bristles. Soft, loose-webbed plumage generally dull brown, gray, or white, sometimes streaked or spotted; often a breast band. Sexes similar.

Habits: Rather stodgy, inactive forest birds that sit motionless for long periods with feathers puffed out and make occasional brief sallies for insects in air or on ground. Nest in ground burrow or tree termite nest. Nesting little studied.

Most are nongregarious, a few are occasionally found in small flocks. Most live entirely on insects; a few also eat fruit. Their flight may be weak or strong, but is seldom for long distances, and is typically undulating. All are hole-nesters; one family is parasitic. Nests with little or no lining. Lay pure-white, roundish eggs; both sexes share nesting chores. Young hatch blind, usually naked, and are nidicolous.

JACAMARS, Galbulidae

Distribution: 15 species, s. Mexico to s. Brazil; rain forests and second growth near forest edges. Nonmigratory.

Characteristics: 5–12″. Wings short, rounded; tail long, often pointed. Bill long, thin, pointed; ridged above and below. Soft, loose-webbed plumage. Usually metallic green, bronze, or purplish above, buffy or black below. Sexes unlike.

Habits: Slender, graceful forest birds that sit quietly on branches and dash out in quick forays for passing insects which they catch on the wing and bring back to the perch. Nest in ground burrows dug by both sexes; lay 3–4 nearly round white eggs.

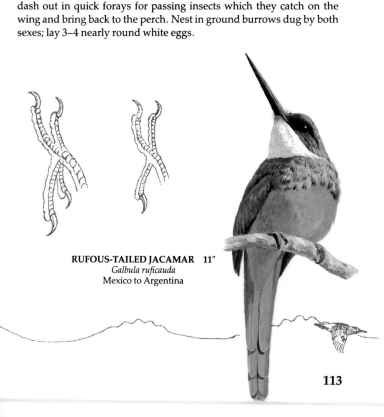

RUFOUS-TAILED JACAMAR   11″
Galbula ruficauda
Mexico to Argentina

BARBETS, Capitonidae

Distribution: 72 species. Costa Rica to Peru and Brazil; Africa south of Sahara; India through Malaysia to Philippines, Sumatra, Borneo. In tropical and subtropical forested grasslands. Nonmigratory.

Characteristics: 3½–12". Wings short, rounded; tail short. Flight weak and seldom sustained. Head large; neck short; body stout. Legs short, stout; feet large. Rictal bristles prominent. Usually bright-colored in greens with bold contrasts of reds, yellow, blues. Bill large, heavy, curved, pointed. Sexes usually alike; both work together at nest building.

Habits: Some mildly gregarious, usually solitary. Treetop birds that sit motionless for hours uttering monotonous, metallic calls; seldom seen on ground. Feed in treetops on insects, fruit, buds. Dig nest holes in trees, termitaria, or stream banks. Usually lay 2–4 eggs; incubation period 13–15 days.

CRIMSON-BREASTED BARBET   7"
Xantholaema haemacephala
Southern Asia, Iran to
the Philippines

HONEYGUIDES, Indicatoridae

Distribution: 11 species. Africa s. of Sahara; 1 species in Himalayas and 1 in Malaysia. In forests, bushy veldt, and savannas. Nonmigratory but show evidence of local seasonal movements.

Characteristics: 4½–8". Wings long, pointed; tail graduated (lyre-shaped in one). Bill short, stout, and blunt, or thin and pointed. Legs rather short; toes and claws strong. Drab birds, brown or gray above, lighter below, yellow patches in some, white spots in tail in others. Sexes mostly unlike.

Habits: Usually solitary, arboreal birds. Flight swift, straight, or undulating. Voices harsh chatter, loud whistle, croaking, squawking. Lead animals (including man) to bees' nests. Honeyguides interest in bees' nest is the wax rather than the honey. All species exhibit brood parasitism so far as known, usually on barbets or woodpeckers. Destroy the eggs of the nest's rightful owner and deposit their own. Nestlings have sharp hook on bill to kill nest mates.

LYRE-TAILED HONEYGUIDE 8"
Melichneutes robustus
Central Africa

GREEN ARACARI 13″
Pteroglossus viridis
Venezuela through Brazil

TOUCANS, Ramphastidae

Distribution: 37 species, s. Mexico to n. Argentina and Paraguay; in rain forest, wooded foothills. Vertical migration in some species.

Characteristics: 12–24″. Wings short, rounded; tail long, rounded to graduated. Tremendous bill, sometimes as large as body, often varicolored, with nostrils at base. Bare skin about eye. Legs and feet stout, strong. Coarse plumage black (green in some) with bold patches of white, red, yellow, or blue. Sexes usually alike.

Habits: Semi-gregarious, especially when feeding with sentry posted; eat fruit, insects, birds' eggs. Voice, short, harsh croaks and calls, often noisy. Nest in tree cavities. Young have prominent heel pads.

GRAY-BREASTED MOUNTAIN TOUCAN 18″
Andigena hypoglauca
Colombia, Ecuador, Peru

CHESTNUT-MANDIBLED TOUCAN 22″
Ramphastos swainsonii
Honduras to Ecuador and Venezuela

SPOT-BILLED TOUCANET 12″
Selenidera maculirostris
Venezuela, Guyana to N. Argentina

117

WOODPECKERS, WRYNECKS, PICULETS, Picidae

Distribution: 213 species, 209 living, 32 fossil, to Pliocene of Kansas. Worldwide except polar regions, Australia, New Zealand, Madagascar, oceanic islands; in forest of all types, a few in open savannas. Most non-migratory.

Characteristics: 3½–22″. Wings long, pointed; tail feathers pointed, usually stiff. Legs short; toes 4 or 3, with long, curved claws. Bill chisel-like, strong, pointed. Colors varied–black and white, browns, greens, with red or yellow head markings; some streaked, spotted, barred; some crested. Sexes usually unlike.

Habits: Rather solitary birds that climb tree trunks and peck bark and wood for insects and grubs. A few dig in earth and feed on ground. Voices loud, harsh; drum with bills. Chisel nest in trees or bank.

GREAT SPOTTED WOODPECKER 9″
Picoides major
Eurasia

THREE-TOED WOODPECKER 9″
Picoides tridactylus
Northern North America and Eurasia

NORTHERN FLICKER 13″
Colaptes auratus
Temperate North America

EURASIAN WRYNECK 7″
Jynx torquilla
Temperate Eurasia

CRIMSON-WINGED WOODPECKER 10″
Picus puniceus
Malaysia

ANTILLEAN PICULET 5″
Nesoctites micromegas
Island of Hispaniola

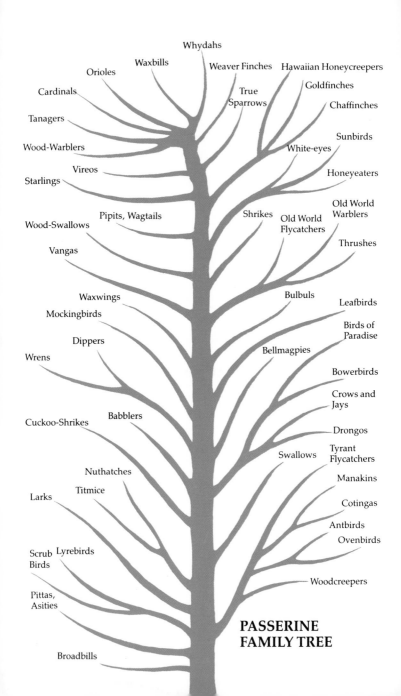

Whydahs
Waxbills
Orioles
Cardinals
Tanagers
Wood-Warblers
Vireos
Starlings
Pipits, Wagtails
Wood-Swallows
Vangas
Waxwings
Mockingbirds
Dippers
Wrens
Cuckoo-Shrikes
Babblers
Nuthatches
Titmice
Larks
Scrub Birds
Lyrebirds
Pittas, Asities
Broadbills

Weaver Finches
True Sparrows
Shrikes
Bellmagpies
Swallows

Hawaiian Honeycreepers
Goldfinches
Chaffinches
Sunbirds
White-eyes
Honeyeaters
Old World Flycatchers
Old World Warblers
Thrushes
Bulbuls
Leafbirds
Birds of Paradise
Bowerbirds
Crows and Jays
Drongos
Tyrant Flycatchers
Manakins
Cotingas
Antbirds
Ovenbirds
Woodcreepers

PASSERINE FAMILY TREE

PERCHING BIRDS—Passeriformes

An immense, complex order of some 60 families containing about 5,200 species, roughly three fifths of the known living birds. Found on all the major land masses of the world except Antarctica and on most oceanic islands capable of supporting bird life. Their diagnostic characteristic is their perching feet, with four unwebbed toes joined at the same level, three in front, one behind.

The perching birds also may be recognized by internal anatomical characters they share, a distinctive palate, a unique type of spermatozoa, and a reduced number of neck vertebrae. All have altricial young that hatch naked (or nearly so) and helpless; reared in the nest.

BROADBILLS, Eurylaimidae

Distribution: 14 species, c. and s. Africa, India e. to s. China, Philippines, s. to Sumatra, Borneo; in wet jungles. Nonmigratory.

Characteristics: 5–11″. Wings short or long, rounded; tail very short, square, or long and pointed. Bill usually wide, flat, heavy, hooked, covered by crest in some species. Chunky birds with large heads, short necks, stout bodies, large eyes. Plumage soft, silky in Asiatic species; African forms duller. Sexes usually unlike.

Habits: Solitary or gregarious arboreal birds; rather tame, unsuspicious; some crepuscular. Sedentary; movements restricted. Live on insects, fruit, berries, frogs, lizards. Eggs 2–8 in large pear-shaped hanging nest, with side entrance.

BLACK-AND-RED BROADBILL 8½″
Cymbirhynchus macrorhynchus
Malaysia

OVENBIRDS, Furnariidae

Distribution: 217 species, s. Mexico to Patagonia; in forest, brushlands, pampas, mountains, semideserts. Most nonmigratory.

Characteristics: 5–11″. Wings short, rounded to long, pointed. Tail short to long, rounded to pointed. Legs short to medium; front toes joined at base. Bill slender, short to long, pointed. Most are brownish above, lighter below, often with contrasting white throats. Some spotted, streaked with black, white, rufous. Sexes alike or nearly so.

Habits: Gregarious or solitary, terrestrial or arboreal. Flight weak to strong, but seldom extended. Terrestrial species walk; a few climb tree trunks. Two pairs syrinx muscles; voices harsh, scolding, loud whistles, trills. Eggs 2–6, usually white, in great variety of nests–domed of mud or grass; in reeds, brushes, on ground or hole in ground, rocks, trees. Incubation and care by both parents.

RUFOUS OVENBIRD   8″
Furnarius rufus
Argentina and southern Brazil

PEARLED TREERUNNER   6½″
Margarornis squamiger
Venezuela to Peru and Bolivia

BLACK-BANDED WOODCREEPER 11"
Dendrocolaptes picumnus
Guatemala to Argentina

RED-BILLED WOODCREEPER 12"
Hylexetastes perrotii
Venezuela through Brazil

WOODCREEPERS, Dendrocolaptidae

Distribution: 48 species. Mexico to n. Argentina; in forest, brushlands.

Characteristics: 5½–14". Wings long, rounded; tail long, rounded or graduated, with stiff, sharp-pointed shafts. Legs short; feet and claws strong; front toes joined at base. Bill short and straight to long and downcurved; laterally compressed. Plumage dull brown, variously streaked, mottled, barred buff, gray, black, white. Sexes alike.

Habits: Solitary or in pairs, sometimes in mixed flocks of other species. Fly strongly from tree to tree. Climb trunk probing for insects; prop with tails. Voice, repetitive calls, flutey trills, harsh nasal notes (only 2 pairs syrinx muscles). Nest in tree cavities; 2–3 white eggs; incubation and natal care by both sexes.

123

ANTBIRDS, Formicariidae

Distribution: 231 species, s. Mexico to Paraguay and n. Argentina; in forests, brushlands. Nonmigratory.

Characteristics: 4–14″. Wings short, rounded; tail short to long; legs short to long. Front toes slightly joined at base. Bill stoutish, always hooked at tip, strongly so in some. Loose-webbed plumage dull colored, patterned inconspicuously in drab browns, grays, blacks. Sexes usually unlike.

Habits: Solitary or in pairs, a few in small bands. Arboreal or terrestrial. Flight weak. Food insects, which many species find by following columns of army ants. Distinctive calls, low songs, whistled notes (syrinx muscles 1 or 2). Usually 2, rarely 3, eggs, in open cup nest in bush or low tree or on ground. Incubation and parental care by both sexes.

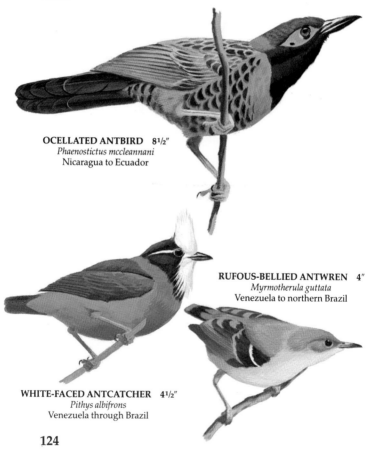

OCELLATED ANTBIRD 8¹/₂″
Phaenostictus mccleannani
Nicaragua to Ecuador

RUFOUS-BELLIED ANTWREN 4″
Myrmotherula guttata
Venezuela to northern Brazil

WHITE-FACED ANTCATCHER 4¹/₂″
Pithys albifrons
Venezuela through Brazil

124

BARRED ANTSHRIKE   6″
Thamnophilus doliatus
Mexico to Argentina

RUFOUS-CAPPED ANTTHRUSH   7¹/₂″
Formicarius colma
Venezuela to Brazil,
Peru, Ecuador

BLACK-BREASTED GNATEATER   5¹/₂″
Conopophaga melanogaster
Central Brazil and Bolivia

BROWN-BANDED ANTPITTA   6¹/₂″
Grallaria milleri
Colombia

TAPACULOS, Rhinocryptidae

Distribution: 27 species. Mountains of Costa Rica, down Andes chain to Patagonia; dry, barren hillsides s. Brazil to Terra del Fuego. Nonmigratory.

Characteristics: 4¹/₂–10″. Wings short, rounded; tail short to medium. Bill stout, pounted. Legs and feet stout, strong. Nostrils covered with movable flap. Stout bodied, with soft, loose plumage; somber browns, grays, often patterned with red-browns and black. Sexes alike.

Habits: Solitary (forest species) to somewhat gregarious. Terrestrial birds that walk or run fast with tail held erect; fly weakly and seldom. Food, insects, some seeds, buds. Some scratch the ground litter like chickens. Eggs 2–4, white, in ground nest or burrow, or in domed nest in low bush. Natal care by both parents. Little known of nesting.

BLACK-THROATED HUET HUET
Pteroptochos tarnii
Western Argentina and Chile

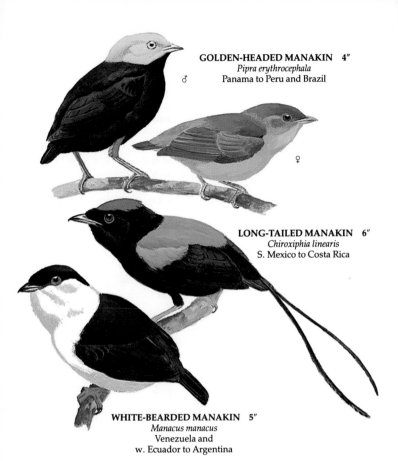

GOLDEN-HEADED MANAKIN 4″
Pipra erythrocephala
♂ Panama to Peru and Brazil
♀

LONG-TAILED MANAKIN 6″
Chiroxiphia linearis
S. Mexico to Costa Rica

WHITE-BEARDED MANAKIN 5″
Manacus manacus
Venezuela and
w. Ecuador to Argentina

MANAKINS, Pipridae

Distribution: 59 species, s. Mexico to Paraguay, n. Argentina; in woodlands. Nonmigratory.

Characteristics: 3½–6½″. Wings short, rounded; tail short and stubby (elongated in a few). Legs short, slender; front toes partly joined at base. Bill broad, pointed, slightly hooked. Males usually solid brown or black with bright patches of red, yellow, blue, on head, back, thighs. Females typically greenish.

Habits: Solitary or in small bands. Fly fast and straight for short distances. Feed on berries, insects. Calls simple, low chirps, whistles. Some make buzzing noises with wings. Males polygamous. Eggs 2 in frail cup nest in branch fork. Incubation and natal care by female.

TYRANT FLYCATCHERS, Tyrannidae

Distribution: 367 species, throughout temperate and tropical Western Hemisphere, Canadian tree line to Patagonia, forest, plains. Temperate species migratory.

Characteristics: 3½–16″. Wings short to long and pointed; tail medium, rounded or forked. Legs and feet small, weak (except in a few terrestrial species). Head largish; bill typically broad, flat, hooked at tip. Plumage typically plain olive-green, brown, or gray. Sexes alike except in the few bright-colored species.

Habits: Typically solitary, arboreal. Most feed by catching insects on the wing in short sallies from a prominent perch. Perching stance upright. Distinctive calls, but song poorly developed. Eggs 2–6, white, clear or marked. Incubation usually by female, but male helps build nest and feed young.

TROPICAL KINGBIRD 9″
Tyrannus melancholicus
Southwestern U.S. to Argentina

EASTERN WOOD-PEWEE 6½″
Contopus virens
Eastern North America

GREAT CRESTED FLYCATCHER 9″
Myiarchus crinitus
Eastern North America

ACADIAN FLYCATCHER 6″
Empidonax virescens
Eastern United States

SPOTTED TODY FLYCATCHER 4″
Todirostrum maculatum
Venezuela to Brazil and Bolivia

YELLOW-BELLIED ELAENIA 7″
Elaenia flavogaster
Mexico to Argentina

COTINGAS, Cotingidae

Distribution: 91 species, s. Arizona, Texas s. to Paraguay, n. Argentina. Also Jamaica. In rain forests, highland forest. Most nonmigratory.

Characteristics: 3½–18″. Wings short, rounded to fairly long; tail short to long. Legs short; feet large. Bill short to long, often flattened. Great variation in color, form. Some crested, some with bare patches on face, some wattled. Many gray or brown, simply patterned. Some white, black, red, purple green. Sexes alike and unlike.

Habits: Mostly solitary arboreal birds (cock-of-the-rock, terrestrial) that live on fruit and insects. Flight medium to fairly strong. Voices varied; loud, metallic peals, shrill whistles, unbirdlike noises, etc. Eggs 1–6; in tree cavity, large covered nest in tree, shallow cup on branch, or mud nest on rock wall. Incubation by female. Natal care by both.

PURPLE-BREASTED COTINGA 8″
Cotinga cotinga
Southern Venezuela
to northern Brazil

SCARLET-BREASTED FRUITEATER 8″
Pipreola frontalis
Ecuador, Peru, northern Bolivia

BLACK-TAILED TITRA 9″
Tityra cayana
Venezuela and Ecuador to Argentina

COCK-OF-THE-ROCK 13″
Rupicola rupicola
Guyana, Surinam, French Guiana,
and northern Brazil

LESSER BECARD 8″
Platypsaris minor
Venezuela and Ecuador
to Brazil and Bolivia

**BRIGHT-RUMPED
ATTILA** 8″
Attila spadiceus
Mexico to Brazil,
Bolivia, Peru

131

SHARPBILL, Oxyruncidae

Distribution: 1 species, Costa Rica, Panama, Venezuela, Guyana, s.e. Brazil, Paraguay; in rain forest. Probably permanently residential rather than migratory.

Characteristics: 6½–7″. Close to tyrants, but bill sharp-pointed, unhooked; feet stouter; rictal bristles replaced by fine bristly feathers; nostril elongate instead of round, covered with flap. Olive-green above; bright red crest partly concealed (paler in female); spotted yellowish-white below. Sexes similar.

Habits: Solitary fruit-eaters that fly strongly. Voice, breeding habits unreported. Behavior poorly known.

SHARPBILL 7″
Oxyruncus cristatus
Costa Rica to Paraguay

RUFOUS-TAILED PLANTCUTTER 6″
Phytotoma rara
W. Argentina and Chile

PLANTCUTTERS, Phytotomidae

Distribution: 3 species, w. Peru to Patagonia; open woodlands, brushlands, cultivated areas. Partly migratory.

Characteristics: 6½–7″. Wings short, pointed; tail longish. Legs short; feet large; bill short, conical, strong, serrate-edged. Gray or brown above, rufous-red below, wings and tail black. Body stocky. Sexes unlike.

Habits: Solitary or small flocks. Flight weak, undulating, unsustained. Eat fruit, leaves, buds; destructive to crops. Calls harsh, unmusical. Eggs 2–4, blue-green spotted brown, in open nest in bush or tree. Incubation by female alone; young fed by both.

PITTAS, Pittidae

Distribution: 23 species, s. Africa, India to Japan, East Indies to Australia and Solomons; in forest, brushlands. Some species migratory.

Characteristics: 6–11". Wings short, rounded; tail very short; legs and feet long, strong; bill stout, slightly downcurved. Body stout; neck short. Loose-webbed plumage in bright, contrasting colors in solid patches. Females usually duller.

Habits: Solitary, terrestrial. Fly strongly, straight. Hop on ground. Food, earthworms, insects, small animals. Perch and roost in trees. Calls, loud, varied. Eggs 2–7, white to buffy, spots. Large loose globular nest on, near ground. Both sexes incubate and care for altricial young.

HOODED PITTA 7"
Pitta sordida cucullata
Himalayas through Indochina to
New Guinea

BLUE-HEADED PITTA 9"
Pitta baudi
Malaysia

133

ASITIES, Philepittidae

Distribution: 4 species; Madagascar forests. Nonmigratory.

Characteristics: 3½–6½". Wings and tail short, rounded. Legs and feet large, strong, or small, weak. Bill short, slender, slightly curved, or long, thin, strongly downcurved. Plumage soft; black with yellow on wing, or blue and yellow. Bare or wattled orbital space. Sexes unlike.

Habits: Solitary or in pairs. Arboreal. Asities quiet, stolid, tame; fly strongly but not far. Eat fruit, berries. Soft, thrush-like song. Eggs 3, in pear-shaped hanging nest. False Sunbirds dip into flowers for nectar and small insects. Breeding unknown.

RIFLEMAN 3"
Acanthisitta chloris
New Zealand

VELVET ASITY 6½"
Philepitta castanea
Eastern Madagascar

NEW ZEALAND WRENS, Acanthisittidae

Distribution: 4 species, 3 living, 1 lately extinct. In New Zealand forests and scrublands. Nonmigratory.

Characteristics: 3–4". Wings and tail short; legs and feet long, slender. Bill pointed, slender. Soft plumage, brownish or yellowish green, black wings and tail, white eye-stripe. Sexes unlike.

Habits: Solitary or in small bands. Very weak fliers, but run actively around rocks, tree branches in search of insects and larvae. Eggs 2–5, white, in covered nest in tree crevice or hole in earth, rocks, log. Simple chips, calls; no true song.

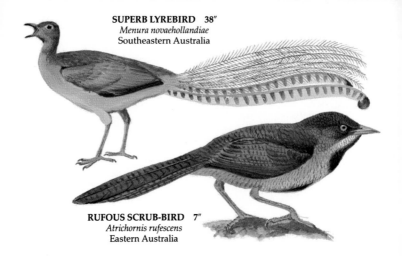

SUPERB LYREBIRD 38″
Menura novaehollandiae
Southeastern Australia

RUFOUS SCRUB-BIRD 7″
Atrichornis rufescens
Eastern Australia

LYREBIRDS, Menuridae

Distribution: 2 species, in montane forest of southeastern Australia. Nonmigratory.

Characteristics: 30–40″. Wings short, rounded; tail long, very fancy in male. Legs and feet large and strong. Bill conical, sharp-pointed. Neck longish. Plumage dark brown above, ashy brown below; bare bluish space around eye. Sexes unlike.

Habits: Solitary, terrestrial, but roost in trees. Fly seldom, but can glide some distance. Run and leap with great speed through underbrush. Eat insects, worms, land crustaceans and mollusks. Varied notes and calls; incredible mimics of any sound they hear. Males polygamous. Egg 1, dark gray with inky markings, in bulky, domed nest. Incubation and care of young by female alone.

SCRUB-BIRDS, Atrichornithidae

Distribution: 2 species, thick brush and scrublands of southwestern and eastern Australia. Nonmigratory.

Characteristics: 7–8½″. Wings very short, rounded; tail long, graduated. Legs and feet large, strong. Bill medium, rounded, pointed. Plumage red-brown above, lighter below, with fine black markings. Sexes similar.

Habits: Solitary, terrestrial, almost flightless birds, that scuttle speedily through tangled vines and undergrowth, holding tail erect. Very shy, retiring. Eat snails, worms, inserts, occasional seeds. Loud ringing calls, good mimics. Lay 2 pinkish-white eggs with brown markings in loosely-woven domed nest on or near ground. Incubation and natal care by female alone.

135

LARKS, Alaudidae

Distribution: 78 species, 75 living, 11 fossil, to Pliocene of Italy. Eurasia, Africa, Australia, North America to s. Mexico, n.w. South America. Open grassy plains, moors, fields, beaches. Many migratory.

Characteristics: 5–9″. Wings long, pointed; tail medium; fairly long legs, with long, straight claw on hind toe; back of tarsus rounded and scaled. Bill pointed, slightly downcurved. Typically brown to gray-buff above, patterned cryptically with dark brown, black; lighter below. Sexes similar.

Habits: Fairly gregarious terrestrial birds that fly strongly and walk on the ground. Food insects, larvae, seeds. Most sing beautifully; a soaring flight song in many. Eggs 2–6, spotted or clear white. Incubation mostly by female. Male feeds her on nest and helps feed young.

†PALEOSPIZA, Paleospizidae

A single species of primitive passerine from the Oligocene of Colorado.

EURASIAN SKYLARK 7″
Alauda arvensis
Eurasia, northern Africa

HORNED LARK 7″
Eremophila alpestris
Eurasia, n. Africa, North America,
Mexico, Colombia

136

TREE SWALLOW 5¹/₂″
Tachycineta bicolor
North America

BARN SWALLOW 7¹/₂″
Hirundo rustica
Eurasia, North America

SWALLOWS, Hirundinidae

Distribution: 80 species, 79 living, 9 fossil to Pleistocene of Rumania. Worldwide except polar regions and some oceanic islands. Migratory.

Characteristics: 4–9″. Wings very long, pointed; tail medium to long, truncate to forked. Legs very short; feet small, weak. Bill short, flat, but gape wide, enhanced by rictal bristles. Plumage compact, usually darker above than below, often with some metallic sheen. Sexes alike or nearly so in most species.

Habits: Gregarious and well-loved insectivorous birds that spend much of their waking hours flying. Flight strong, agile; walk with difficulty. Feed on the wing. Nest usually colonially, in hollows in trees or rocks, or burrows dug in banks, or build mud nests. Eggs 3–7, white, clear or marked. Incubated by both sexes or female alone. Male always helps feed young.

CROWS AND JAYS, Corvidae

Distribution: 112 species, 102 living, 31 fossil to Miocene of France. Almost cosmopolitan. Absent from Antarctica, some oceanic islands, southern South America. Varied habitats, prefer woodlands and open brushlands. Most nonmigratory.

Characteristics: 8–28". Mostly medium to large-sized. Crows, which include the largest of the passerines, are black, or black and gray or white; wings long and pointed; tail much shorter than wing. Jays usually smaller, often bright-colored in blues, greens, yellows; wings shorter, rounded; tail sometimes longer than wings. Tarsus large, strongly scutellate, booted behind. Rictal bristles present; nostrils usually feathered. Large 10th (outer) primary. Sexes alike.

Habits: Bold, inquisitive, highly adaptable birds. Often gregarious. Voices loud, harsh. Food habits omnivorous, somewhat predatory. Hold food with feet, break it with beak. Open nest in trees or on cliffs. Eggs 3–10, usually greenish and speckled; some white. Nest building and care of young by both sexes; incubation and brooding by female alone.

COMMON RAVEN 26"
Corvus corax
Eurasia, North America

138

BLACK-BILLED MAGPIE 18″
Pica pica
Eurasia, western North America

EURASIAN JAY 13″
Garrulus glandarius
Temperate Eurasia

CLARK'S NUTCRACKER 12″
Nucifraga columbiana
Rocky Mountains

BIRDS OF PARADISE, Paradisaeidae

Distribution: 40 species. Moluccas, New Guinea and adjacent islands, n. and e. Australia; in forests. Nonmigratory.

Characteristics: 5½–42″. Small to medium-sized birds, highly variable in color, but glossy black and metallic hues predominate in males, most of which have spectacular plumes on neck, breast, flanks, tail, or wing; some have wattles or bare tracts on head. Females unornamented drab browns or grays. Bills medium and jay-like to long, slender, downcurved. Wings medium, rounded; legs short; feet fairly stout.

Habits: Solitary arboreal birds, not strong fliers. Eat fruit, seeds, insects, small vertebrates. Males have spectacular courtship displays; some species polygamous. Nest usually cup-shaped, of plant materials in tree; eggs 2, typically heavily streaked longitudinally. Incubation by female alone; male helps feed young in a few species.

GREATER BIRD OF PARADISE 18″
Paradisaea apoda
New Guinea

♂

♀

LITTLE KING BIRD OF PARADISE 7″
Cicinnurus regius
New Guinea

WILSON'S BIRD OF PARADISE 6¹/₂″
Diphyllodes respublica
New Guinea

**TWELVE-WIRED
BIRD OF PARADISE** 13″
Seleucidis ignotus
New Guinea

MAGNIFICENT BIRD OF PARADISE 8″
Diphyllodes magnificus
New Guinea

141

SATIN BOWERBIRD 13″
Ptilonorhynchus violaceus
Eastern Australia

BOWERBIRDS, Ptilonorhynchidae

Distribution: 17 species, New Guinea and n. Australia; in forests. Non-migratory.

Characteristics: 9–15″. Medium-sized, 10-primaried oscines of varied colors, sometimes brilliant in males; some with pronounced nuchal crests, but never with plumes or head wattles. Hind toe shorter than middle front toe. Sexes alike in a few species.

Habits: Largely solitary and terrestrial. Essentially omnivorous; feed on ground and in trees on berries, seeds, fruits, small invertebrates. Voices loud, ringing; some fine mimics. Males build elaborate "bowers" or "stages" for display and courtship. Nest a loose, open cup in trees or vines, built by female alone. Eggs 1–3, usually 2, pure white or with brown markings. Male assists in care of young in a few species, but usually continues to display long after mating.

142

BELLMAGPIES, Cracticidae

Distribution: 10 species, Australia, New Guinea, adjacent islands; in open forests, brushy plains, cleared lands, mangrove seashores. Non-migratory.

Characteristics: 10–22″. Medium to large oscines; mostly black, gray, and white; a few have brown phases. Bill large, straight, slightly to strongly hooked; nostrils bare; legs medium to long, semi-booted; wings long, pointed. Sexes alike or different.

Habits: Usually gregarious, arboreal, often feed on ground. Eat insects, small vertebrates, some fruit and seeds. Butcherbirds impale prey on thorns in shrike fashion. Nest a large open cup of twigs lined with soft material, high in tree. Eggs 3–5; highly variable; incubated mainly by female. Natal care by both sexes.

BLACK-THROATED BUTCHERBIRD   13″
Cracticus nigrogularis
Australia

MUDNEST-BUILDERS, Grallinidae

Distribution: 4 species, Australia, w. New Guinea; in open woodlands, marshes, farmlands, usually near water. Some migratory.

Characteristics: 8–20″. 10-primaried oscines with no nasal bristles and unbooted tarsus. Magpie-larks boldly black and white; thrush-sized; graceful inhabitants of stream banks, lake shore; eat insects, mollusks. Apostle-bird dark gray, jay-sized dweller of woods and croplands. Feeds largely on ground on insects and seeds. White-winged Chough glossy black; crow-sized; open land dweller; eats insects and soft fruit. Sexes alike and unlike.

Habits: All somewhat gregarious; poor fliers, with peculiar jumping gait. All build deep, bowl-shaped nests of mud strengthened with hair, grass, feathers, usually on high tree branch. Eggs 3–8, white, marked with brown, black. Incubation and care of young by both sexes.

MAGPIE-LARK   11″
Grallina cyanoleuca
Australia

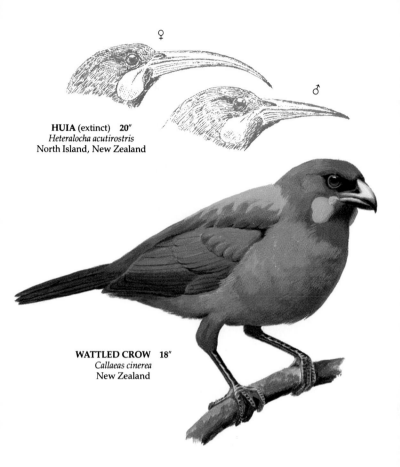

HUIA (extinct) **20″**
Heteralocha acutirostris
North Island, New Zealand

♀

♂

WATTLED CROW 18″
Callaeas cinerea
New Zealand

WATTLEBIRDS, Callaeidae

Distribution: 3 species, 2 living, 1 lately extinct. New Zealand primeval forests. Nonmigratory. Huia extinct; Wattled Crow, Saddleback rare.

Characteristics: 10–21″. Plain black, brown, or blue-gray birds with orange or blue wattles at gape. Sexes differ in size, bill shape, and wattles. Bill stout and short to long and curved. Legs long; feet strong. Wings short, rounded; tail long.

Habits: Weak fliers, but hop actively over ground and from branch to branch. Eat insects, fruit, nectar. Cup-shaped nest of sticks lined with moss, grass, feathers; on ground or low in trees. Eggs 2–3, gray, marked with brown. Both sexes tend young.

145

LESSER RACKET-TAILED DRONGO   11″
Dicrurus hottentottus
India to Southeast Asia, Malaysia

DRONGOS, Dicruridae

Distribution: 20 species, Africa, s. Asia, Philippines to Solomons, Malaysia, n. Australia; in forests, cultivated lands, wooded savannas. Some species migratory.

Characteristics: 7–25″. Small to medium-sized, typically black with green to purple iridescenses (1 species gray); often crested or with spangled head and neck feathers. Wings long; tail medium to very long, usually forked, outer feathers often elongate. Bill stout, arched, slightly hooked and notched. Legs short; feet stout. Sexes alike.

Habits: Nongregarious, active, arboreal birds that fly strongly and undulatingly but seldom long or far. Food predominantly insects caught in flight; hawk from perch; follow cattle or monkey troops for insects they disturb. Pugnacious; defend territory by attacking larger birds fearlessly. Voice melodious, varied; mimic other birds. Saucer-like nest usually in fork of branch. Eggs 3–4, often white spotted with brown. Incubation largely by female. Both sexes tend young.

FOREST ORIOLES, Oriolidae

Distribution: 28 species, Eurasia, Africa, East Indies, Philippines, Australia; in forests, semi-wooded croplands, seldom in open. Some migratory.

Characteristics: 8–12″. Bright-colored birds with yellows, greens, and black predominating. Wings long, pointed; tail medium to long. Bill strong, pointed, slightly hooked. Legs short; feet stout. Sexes usually unlike; female duller.

Habits: Mostly solitary, arboreal birds; remain hidden in foliage where more often heard than seen. Voices loud, calls harsh, songs melodious. Feed on insects, fruit. Flight strong, undulating. Nest a deep cup, high in tree. Eggs 2–5, variously colored. Incubation mainly by female. Males assist in some. Both sexes rear young.

BLACK-NAPED ORIOLE 10″
Oriolus chinensis
India and Manchuria to the
Philippines and Sulawesi

YELLOW FIGBIRD 10″
Sphecotheres flaviventris
Northern Australia

TITMICE, Paridae

Distribution: 65 species, 64 living, 9 fossil, to Eocene of France. North America, s. to Guatemala; Eurasia, Philippines, Africa; in forests, brushlands. Most nonmigratory.

Characteristics: 3½–8″. Small, friendly birds with soft, thick plumage usually boldly patterned (never streaked, barred, spotted) in grays, browns, yellows, black or white. Bill short, stout, pointed; legs short, strong; wings short to medium, rounded; tail short to long. Sexes usually alike.

Habits: Gregarious, active, curious, unafraid; travel through branches in small mixed flocks, feeding on small insects, some seeds. Whistled calls, chattering notes. Build large, bulky nest of grass, moss, hair, feathers, in tree hollows, rock cavities; some build pendant purselike structures. Eggs 4–15, usually white, plain or spotted. Incubation usually by female alone. Both parents feed young.

LONG-TAILED TIT 6½″
Aegithalos caudatus
Eurasia

BLUE TIT 4½″
Parus caeruleus
Europe, Asia Minor

PENDULINE TIT 4½″
Remiz pendulinus
Eurasia

CREEPERS, Certhiidae

Distribution: 6 species, temperate wooded portions of North America, Eurasia and Africa. Most species migratory.

Characteristics: 5–6". Slender, climbing birds; brownish above streaked with black, white, or lighter brown; white below, with long, stiff, pointed tail feathers. Bill slender, pointed, downcurved; legs short, slender; toes thin; claws long, sharp. Sexes alike.

Habits: Solitary arboreal (except two rock inhabitants) birds; climb tree trunks, usually spiraling upwards from base, probing bark for insects; rarely eat seeds. Nest a hammock-shaped cup usually behind a piece of loose bark. Eggs 4–8, usually 5–6, white with fine red brown spots. Incubation chiefly by female; both parents feed young. Often doublebrooded.

149

NUTHATCHES AND ALLIES, Sittidae

Distribution: 27 species, typically Holarctic, aberrant forms in Africa, Philippines, Australo-Papuan region. In forests; a few in rocky semiarid areas. Mostly nonmigratory.

Characteristics: 3½–7½". Typically small, stocky, short-necked birds; mainly gray to blue above, white or brownish below; top of head often black or brown with dark eye line. Bill thin, pointed, straight; down-curved in Wall Creeper; tarsus short; toes long, strong; wings fairly long, pointed; tail short, square. Sexes alike.

Habits: Solitary arboreal birds (two species live on rocky cliffs). Forage for insects, seeds, small fruits on trunks and larger limbs of trees, climbing up, down, sideways, in short hops, often head downward. Nest in tree hollows or rock cavities, lined with moss, leaves, feathers, hair. Eggs 4–10, white marked with brown; incubated by female alone; young fed by both parents.

WALL CREEPER 6½"
Tichodroma muraria
Central Eurasia

RED-BREASTED NUTHATCH 4½"
Sitta canadensis
Northern North America

RED-BROWED TREECREEPER 5½"
Climacteris erythrops
Eastern Australia

AUSTRALIAN TREECREEPERS, Climacteridae

Distribution: 6 species in Australian forest lands, 1 extending into New Guinea montane forests. Nonmigratory.

Characteristics: 5–7". Small, creeper-like birds; uniform gray-brown to black above, streaked below; often a lighter wing bar and eye stripe. Bill long, downcurved; tail rounded, soft; toes and claws long, strong, curved. Sexes similar but distinguishable.

Habits: Rather sedentary and nongregarious; feed by spiraling upwards around tree trunks; some forage on ground for insects among fallen trunks and limbs. Call, a high-pitched whistle. Nest, deep in tree or stump hollows, lined with plant material and animal fur. Eggs 1–4, white spotted with brown; care of young by both parents.

150

CUCKOO-SHRIKES, Campephagidae

Distribution: 70 species. Africa, India to Japan, East Indies, Australia, e. to Samoa. In forest. Largely nonmigratory.

Characteristics: 5–14″. Largely plain gray, black, or white birds with barred underparts; minivets more brightly colored in reds, yellows. Sexes usually unlike; females brownish. Plumage soft, fluffy, with dense thick patch of loosely attached feathers on lower back. Bill stoutish, downcurved, notched and hooked at tip; nostrils partly hidden by short bristles. Wings medium, pointed; tail long, graduated or rounded. Legs shortish; feet rather weak.

Habits: Gregarious or solitary; largely arboreal birds; fly strongly for short distances. Often noisy; voice, whistles and harsh notes. Eat insects, small fruits, berries. Nest a smallish shallow cup on a horizontal branch. Eggs 2–4, variously colored; incubation and natal care by both sexes.

GROUND CUCKOO-SHRIKE   14″
Pteropodocys maxima
Australia

FLAMED MINIVET   9″
Pericrocotus flammeus
India to Philippines and Borneo

WHITE-CHEEKED BULBUL 7"
Pycnonotus leucogenys
Asia Minor, northern India

BLACK-CRESTED
YELLOW BULBUL 7"
Pycnonotus melanicterus
India through Southeast Asia to Borneo

BULBULS, Pycnonotidae

Distribution: 119 species. Africa, s. Asia to Japan, Philippines, Moluccas, Borneo. In forests, brushlands, cultivated areas. Northern ones migratory.

Characteristics: 6–11". Medium-sized birds with soft, fluffy plumage, especially on lower back; hairlike feathers on nape; rictal bristles well developed. Wings short; tail medium to long; legs and feet small; bill slender, slightly downcurved. Colors usually dull brown, gray, greenish, some with contrasting yellow, white, or red patches on head and vent. Sexes alike.

Habits: Gregarious, noisy arboreal birds. Seldom come to ground. Active, restless, agile, but flight somewhat weak. Eat mostly fruit and berries, insects in varying quantities. Cup-shaped nest, rather fragile, in bush or tree. Eggs 2–4, white, spotted brown. Incubation and natal care by both sexes.

†PALAEOSCINIS, Palaeoscinidae
One fossil species from Miocene of California.

152

FAIRY BLUEBIRD 10″
Irena puella
India to Southeast Asia and East Indies

GOLDEN-FRONTED LEAFBIRD 8″
Chloropsis aurifrons
India to Annam and Sumatra

IORAS, LEAFBIRDS AND ALLIES, Aegithinidae

Distribution: 14 species. Southeast Asia from India to Philippines, south to Sumatra, Java, Borneo. Reside in forests and cultivated lands. Nonmigratory.

Characteristics: 5–8″. Resemble bulbuls in long, fluffy rump feathers and hairlike feathers on nape, but colors brighter, black or brown with contrasting patches of green or yellow. Bill rather long, curved; legs short, thick; wings short, rounded; tail medium, square to rounded. Sexes unlike.

Habits: Gregarious inhabitants of the forest crown; feed mainly on fruit, seeds, buds, some insects. Usually shy, but active; swift-flying. Voices, loud, musical; good mimics. Cup-shaped nest high in trees. Eggs 2–4, cream to pink spotted with brown. Incubation and natal care by both sexes.

153

WRENS, Troglodytidae

Distribution: 60 species, 59 living, 2 fossil, to Pleistocene of Florida. N. Africa, Eurasia, North America except extreme north, South America. Habitat varied, mostly forest edges and brushlands. Also in rocky slopes, reedy marshes, cactus and desert growth. Northern forms migratory.

Characteristics: 4–9". Small, chunky birds, brownish colors prevailing, usually barred, spotted, streaked with black, white, or other browns. Sexes alike. Bill slender, medium to long, and often decurved. Legs and feet strong; front toes partly joined at base. Wings short, rounded; tail usually short, square to rounded, often cocked up.

Habits: Nongregarious; active, inquisitive. Usually forage near ground in underbrush and tangled root growth. Mainly insectivorous, also eat worms and other small invertebrates. Harsh chattering calls, melodious burbling song. Nest usually crude, bulky, domed when not in cavity. Eggs 2–11. Males do not incubate but help rear young. Some species polygamous. Cock nests.

HOUSE WREN 5"
Troglodytes aedon
Southern Canada to Tierra del Fuego

CANYON WREN 5½"
Catherpes mexicanus
British Columbia to s. Mexico

DIPPERS, Cinclidae

Distribution: 4 species. Eurasia, n. Africa, western Americas from Alaska to Argentina. On swift, rocky streams. Nonmigratory.

Characteristics: 6–8″. Chunky, plain-colored birds, uniform brown, gray, or black; some mottled or with white patches on throat, breast, head, back. Plumage soft, dense, with thick undercoat of down. Wings short, pointed, concave; tail short, square or rounded. Bill slender, straight, laterally compressed; legs and toes rather long, stout, strong. Sexes alike.

Habits: Solitary inhabitants of fast highland streams; dive and swim well under water. Fly straight, fast, close to water. Walk with bobbing gait. Eat insects, aquatic larvae and other organisms. Voice a shrill penetrating whistle, a chattering song. Nest a bulky domed mass of moss with side entrance, among rocks or roots close to water. Eggs 3–7, pure white. Incubation by female alone. Both parents feed young.

COMMON DIPPER   7″
Cinclus cinclus
Europe to Himalayas

VARIEGATED WREN 5"
Malurus lamberti
Southeastern Australia

EMU WREN 7½"
Stipiturus malachurus
S. Australia and Tasmania

WREN-WARBLERS, Maluridae

Distribution: 83 species. Papua, Australia, New Zealand. In woodlands, scrub and heathlands. Nonmigratory.

Characteristics: 3–10". Many are brightly colored in contrasting shiny blues, reds, black, white, with a long tail carried cocked up over back. Bill small, weak; wings short, rounded; legs and feet medium. Sexes alike and unlike.

Habits: Gregarious, active little birds that move through the foliage in small flocks searching for small insects and larvae. Most are good singers; some clever mimics. Nest usually domed with side entrance; a few make open cups of plant fibers and spider webs. Eggs 2–5, whitish with brown markings. Incubation by female alone. Male helps feed young.

WHISTLERS, SHRIKE-THRUSHES, Pachycephalidae

Distribution: 42 species, Australia, New Guinea, Malaya, Philippines, Oceania. In woodlands, shrublands, mangroves, savannas. A few migratory.

Characteristics: 5–11″. Stout-bodied birds with roundish heads, rather heavy bills, some with a shrike-like hooked tip. Most are brown to greenish-gray above, lighter below, often with yellow or dull red markings. Sexes alike and unlike.

Habits: Common, often conspicuous birds usually found singly or in pairs in shrublands or forest edges. Hunt insects among branches and twigs; some also eat fruit. Melodious flutey calls, pairs often duet. Nest a large open cup; eggs 2–4, whitish with brown markings. Incubation and natal care by both sexes.

GOLDEN WHISTLER 7″
Pachycephala pectoralis
Java and Australia to Fiji Islands

WESTERN SHRIKE-THRUSH 9″
Colluricincla rufiventris
Western Australia

OLD WORLD WARBLERS, Muscicapidae, Sylviinae, Sylviini (Tailorbirds, Kinglets, and Chiffchaff)

Distribution: 285 species, 279 living, 10 fossil, to Miocene of France. Worldwide except polar regions, southern South America, and some oceanic islands. Largely in wooded areas, but some in brushlands and marshes. Many migratory.

Characteristics: 3½–10″. Typically small birds with slender, weak bills; short to medium legs; rounded wings of medium length. Colors usually plain drab browns, grays, olive-greens with little pattern; a few are streaked and barred. Sexes alike or nearly so; young never spotted.

Habits: Mostly nongregarious and arboreal; some live in reedy swamps or grassy meadows. Voices varied, pleasant; song well developed in some. Food largely insects and other small animal life. Nest an open cup or domed; in trees, bushes, or reeds; between two leaves in one genus. Eggs 2–10, white to buffy, usually spotted. Incubation by female alone or by both sexes. Young reared by both parents.

REED WARBLER 5″
Acrocephalus scirpaceus
Europe, western Asia

MOUSTACHED WARBLER 5″
Lusciniola melanopogon
S. Europe, Asia Minor

RUPPELL'S WARBLER 5½″
Sylvia ruppelli
Eastern Mediterranean

BLACK-NECKED TAILORBIRD 5″
Orthotomus atrogularis
India through Malaysia

GOLDEN-CROWNED KINGLET 3½″
Regulus sátrapa
North America

BLACK-TAILED GNATCATCHER 5″
Polioptila melanura
Southwestern U.S., northern Mexico

GNATCATCHERS, GNATWRENS, Muscicapidae, Sylviinae, Polioptilini

Distribution: 11 species. Temperate North America southward to Argentina, in open woodlands, semiarid deserts, forest understory. Blue-gray gnatcatcher migratory, others sedentary.

Characteristics: 4–5½″. Dainty, slender little birds with long tails constantly in motion; long, thin, pointed bills. Blue-gray or brown above, lighter below; some have black markings on head; most have white in outer tail feathers. Sexes alike or nearly so.

Habits: Active arboreal birds that forage for insects among outer leaves and twigs of trees and shrubs, usually singly or in pairs. Simple short call notes, songs varied trills and warbles, whispered rather than sung. Compactly woven cup nest of plant down, mosses, lichens, usually straddled on a branch. Eggs 4–5, pale bluish spotted with brown. Incubation and care of young by both sexes.

OLD WORLD FLYCATCHERS, Muscicapidae, Muscicapinae

Distribution: 398 species. Old World from tree line southward, e. in Pacific to Hawaii and Marquesas. In forests, brushlands, agricultural and riparian associations. Many migratory.

Characteristics: 3–9″ (21″ in Paradise Flycatchers). Small birds with broad, flat bills, well developed rictal bristles, rather short, weak legs. Colors varied, some plain grays or browns, others bright blues, reds, chestnuts, or black and white in broad patterns. Some crested; a few with facial wattles. Sexes alike or unlike; young usually spotted.

Habits: Nongregarious arboreal birds that typically feed by sallying forth from a perch to snap insects from the air. Some feed on ground or glean insects from leaves or trunks. Voices varied, but tend to be weak and monotonous. Song well developed in a few. Nest usually a neat cup on a branch or in tree, bank, or ledge cavity. Eggs 2–7, usually heavily spotted. Nest building and incubation by both sexes or by female alone. Care of young by both parents.

PIED FLYCATCHER   5″
Ficedula hypoleuca
Europe, western Asia

RED-CAPPED ROBIN   4¹/₂″
Petroica goodenovii
Australia

SPOTTED FLYCATCHER   5¹/₂″
Muscicapa striata
Eurasia

BLACK PARADISE FLYCATCHER 20"
Terpsiphone atrocaudata
Japan, Ryukyu Islands, Taiwan

JAPANESE BLUE FLYCATCHER 5½"
Cyanoptila cyanomelana
Manchuria, Korea, Japan

BLACK-NAPED BLUE MONARCH 6"
Hypothymis azurea
India to the Philippines and East Indies

THRUSHES, Muscicapidae, Turdinae

Distribution: 305 species, 303 living, 2 lately extinct. Almost cosmopolitan; absent from New Zealand and some other oceanic islands, the Antarctic, and parts of the Arctic. Habitat varied, forest to deserts, farmlands, brushlands, grasslands. Most species migratory.

Characteristics: 4½–13". Small to medium-sized birds with rather slender bills; fairly stout legs and feet; tarsus usually booted; wings rounded to pointed, with 10 primaries. Colors mostly browns, grays, blues, often blended, sometimes in bold patterns with black, white, reds. Sexes alike or unlike; young usually spotted below. One (postnuptial) molt per year.

Habits: Usually solitary birds, but many gregarious on migration and in winter. Mostly arboreal, but many are terrestrial. Food largely insects and fruit; also eat worms, mollusks, seeds, leaves. Song highly developed in most. Nest an open cup of grasses or moss, often lined with mud; in trees or shrubs or on ground; sometimes in rock or tree cavities, rarely in burrows. Nest building, incubation, brooding largely by female; male assists in some species, always helps feed young.

WOOD THRUSH 8"
Hylocichla mustelina
Eastern North America

BLUETHROAT 5½"
Erithacus svecica
Eurasia

BLUE ROCK THRUSH 9"
Monticola solitarius
Southern Eurasia, Spain to Japan

WHITE-STARRED BUSH-ROBIN 10″
Pogonocichla stellata
Tropical Africa

ORANGE-TAILED SHAMA 8″
Copsychus pyrrhopygus
Malaysia

BLACK-EARED WHEATEAR 6″
Oenanthe hispanica
Spain to Iran, n. Africa

AMERICAN ROBIN 10″
Turdus migratorius
North America

163

BABBLERS, Muscicapidae, Timaliinae

Distribution: 257 species. Central and eastern Eurasia, Africa, Madagascar, Philippines, East Indies, Australia. In woodlands, brushlands, scrub areas. Essentially nonmigratory.

Characteristics: 3½–16″. A diverse and poorly defined group of uncertain lineage and affinities. Plumage soft, lax, fluffy; wings short, rounded, concave, close-fitting to body; legs and feet relatively large, strong. Usually dull-colored; a few bright and boldly patterned. Sexes alike and unlike.

Habits: Gregarious or solitary; usually arboreal; some largely terrestrial. Rather weak fliers; tend to be noisy; voices harsh to musical. All insectivorous, eat other small animals, and some fruit. Nest cup-shaped or domed with side entrance; on ground, rock ledges, in grass, bushes, trees. Eggs 2–7, colors various. Incubation by both sexes or female alone. Both parents feed young.

HORSFIELD'S JUNGLE BABBLER 7″
Trichastoma sepiarium
Southeast Asia

RED-HEADED TREE BABBLER 7″
Malacopteron magnum
Malaysia

**CHESTNUT-BACKED
SCIMITAR BABBLER 8″**
Pomatorhinus montanus
Malaysia

GRAY-THROATED TREE BABBLER 5"
Stachyris nigricollis
Himalayas to Malaysia

FLUFFY-BACKED TIT-BABBLER 6"
Macronous ptilosus
Malaysia, Sumatra, Borneo

WHITE-CRESTED LAUGHING THRUSH 12"
Garrulax leucolophus
Himalayas to Southeast Asia

BEARDED TIT 6½"
Panurus biarmicus
Southeastern Europe to Manchuria

WRENTIT 6"
Chamaea fasciata
Oregon to n. Baja California

WRENTIT, Muscicapidae, Timaliinae, Chamaeini

Distribution: 1 species, Oregon to n. Baja California; in brushlands and forest edges. Nonmigratory.

Characteristics: 6½". Thick fluffy plumage, dark slaty brown above, paler and faintly streaked below. Wings short, rounded; tail long, graduated. Bill shortish, rounded, slightly downcurved. Legs and feet strong. Sexes alike.

Habits: Usually found in pairs, more often heard than seen in the thick chaparral. Food insects, small berries. Nest a neat cup in bush near ground. Voice, loud ringing whistles on one pitch. Usually lay 4 eggs of pale blue.Incubation and natal care is provided by both parents.

PARROTBILLS AND BEARDED TITS, Muscicapidae, Panurinae

Distribution: 19 species, temperate Eurasia; in brushy grasslands, scrublands, bamboo thickets. Nonmigratory.

Characteristics: 4–7". Plain little birds, brownish above, lighter below, with short, heavy, laterally compressed bills, short rounded wings, longish graduated tail. Sexes alike or nearly so.

Habits: Gregarious, active; travel through brushlands in small flocks hunting seeds, berries, insects. Work over reed stems and small twigs hanging at odd angles.Nest a deep cup of grasses, hair, spider webs; in bushes or reeds near ground. Eggs white, spotted with brown. Nesting chores by both sexes.

166

NORTHERN MOCKINGBIRD 10½"
Mimus polyglottos
United States and Mexico

CRISSAL THRASHER 12"
Toxostoma dorsale
Southwestern U.S. to central Mexico

MIMINE THRUSHES, Mimidae (Mockingbirds, Thrashers, Catbirds)

Distribution: 31 species. Exclusively American, from s. Canada to s. Argentina and Chile, West Indies, Galápagos. In brushlands, forest edges, hedgerows, shrubbery. High latitude forms migratory.

Characteristics: 8–12". Rather slender birds with long tails and legs; bill medium to long, nearly straight to strongly decurved. Colors brown, gray, or slaty; underparts paler, often white, streaked, or spotted. Some uniformly colored, others with white patches in wings or tail. Sexes alike.

Habits: Solitary or in pairs; strong, versatile singers; many are excellent mimics. Feed on or near ground, in or near brush growth, on insects, fruit, seeds. Nest bulky, cup-shaped, in bushes, low trees, or on ground. Eggs 2–5, green to blue or buff, usually spotted. Male helps in nest building and care of young; rarely incubates.

ACCENTORS (HEDGE-SPARROWS), Prunellidae

Distribution: 12 species. Eurasia and northern edge of Africa. Brushlands, barren mountain slopes to snow line. Migratory, some altitudinally only.

Characteristics: 5–7″. Sparrow-like in appearance, but with slender pointed bill and 10 functional primaries. Colors drab browns, grays; usually streaked and spotted. Sexes similar. Legs and feet strong. Wings medium, rounded to pointed. Tail short, square or emarginate.

Habits: Somewhat gregarious, quiet, unobtrusive birds that feed on or near ground on insects, small invertebrates, berries in summer, seeds in winter. Flight rapid, low, undulating for short distances. Run and hop with shuffling gait accompanied by slight flicks of wings and tail. High metallic calls, thin warbling songs, often in flight. Nest an open cup of grasses, on ground or in low shrub. Eggs 3–4, blue-green, unmarked. Incubation by female or both. Care of young by both.

DUNNOCK 6″
Prunella modularis
Europe, Asia Minor

ALPINE ACCENTOR 7″
Prunella collaris
Eurasian mountains, Spain to Japan

WHITE WAGTAIL 7″
Motacilla alba
Eurasia, Iceland

YELLOW WAGTAIL 7″
Motacilla flava
Eurasia

PIPITS, WAGTAILS, Motacillidae

Distribution: 56 species, 53 living, 9 fossil, to Miocene of France. World-wide except polar regions and oceanic islands. In open prairies, deserts, cultivated fields, open shores. Most species migratory.

Characteristics: 5–9″. Slender-bodied ground birds with thin, pointed bills, rather long, slim legs, elongated hind toes. Pointed wings of 9 primaries; tail typically long and edged white or yellow. Pipit sexes similar; wagtail sexes unlike. Pipits brown, streaked, mottled; wagtails bold patterns of black, white, yellow.

Habits: Gregarious except when nesting. Walk on ground; never hop. Food mainly insects, some vegetable matter. Nest an open cup on ground; sometimes in tree or rock cavity. Eggs 2–7, white or tinted, usually mottled. Incubation by both sexes in wagtails; female alone in pipits, but male helps feed young.

169

WAXWINGS, Bombycillidae

Distribution: 3 species. Subarctic and temperate portions of Northern Hemisphere; in evergreen or birch forest. Migrate nomadically.

Characteristics: 6–7½″. Plumage soft, velvety; in blended drab fawn-browns and grays, secondaries often tipped with waxy red droplets. Sexes similar. Prominent crest. Wings medium, pointed; bill short, thick, slightly hooked.

Habits: Essentially gregarious, arboreal birds that eat mainly berries and fruit, some flowers, buds, insects. Soft lisping calls, weak chattering song. Flight strong, fast, graceful. Nest an open cup in trees. Eggs 3–6, bluish with irregular black or brown spots; incubation largely by female, young fed by both parents.

JAPANESE WAXWING 7″
Bombycilla japonica
Eastern Siberia and Japan

PHAINOPEPLA 7″
Phainopepla nitens
Southwestern U.S. and Mexico

SILKY FLYCATCHERS, Ptilogonatidae

Distribution: 4 species, s.w. U.S. to Panama in arid, brushy country, wet forest edges in Central America. Partly migratory.

Characteristics: 7–9″. Plumage softly silky, solid browns, grays, blacks; crested, two species with yellow markings; white spots in wings and tail. Wings and legs rather short, tail long. Sexes unlike.

Habits: Somewhat gregarious, active, rather shy arboreal birds that live principally on berries and catch insects in flight. Shallow cup nest in a crotch or on a tree limb; eggs 2–4, grayish white spotted black and brown; incubation and natal care by both sexes.

PALM CHAT, Dulidae

Distribution: 1 species. Hispaniola and Gonave Island in West Indies; in open woodlands and cultivated areas. Nonmigratory.

Characteristics: 8″. Plumage stiff and harsh; olive brown above, yellow-white streaked with brown below. Wings medium, rounded; tail longish. Legs and toes stout; bill heavy, laterally compressed. Sexes alike.

Habits: Gregarious arboreal birds that live on fruits and flowers; never feed on ground. Noisy birds with a chorus of harsh chattering. Build large, communal, compartmented nests, in palms or pines, of twigs, sticks, lined with softer bark, grass. Eggs 2–4, white spotted with gray. Natal duties undescribed.

PALM CHAT 8″
Dulus dominicus
Hispaniola

HYPOCOLIUS 7″
Hypocolius ampelinus
Arabia, Iraq

HYPOCOLIUS, Hypocoliidae

Distribution: 1 species, Tigris-Euphrates valley of Iraq, wandering to Afghanistan, western India, Arabia, and coast of Red Sea, in semiarid scrub country, irrigated gardens, palm groves.

Characteristics: 7″. Plumage soft, blue-gray, with black facial, wing, and tail markings and white wingtips. Crested. Sexes alike.

Habits: Rather quiet birds with low-pitched call notes and inferior song. Fly strongly, travel in small flocks, live mostly on fruits. Open cup nest in a thorn bush. Eggs 4–5, milky white, brown spots on large end.

WOOD-SWALLOWS, Artamidae

Distribution: 10 species. Australia north to India, Southeast Asia, Philippines, east to Fiji Islands. In forest clearings or open country with some trees, usually near water. Some species migratory.

Characteristics: 6–8½″. Chunky-bodied birds with long, pointed wings, short squarish tails, short neck, short but strong legs and feet, stout rounded bills. Plumage soft, fine, firm, compact; powder downs present. Plain solid colors, black, gray, or brown above, lighter below. Sexes similar.

Habits: Highly gregarious; roost and take shelter in close-packed clusters. Exceptionally graceful, skillful fliers, able to soar on updrafts. Food, insects caught in flight. Voice a harsh, nasal twittering. Build fragile cup nest in bush or low tree, or in tree or rock cavity. Eggs 2–4, white, spotted. Nesting duties shared by both sexes.

DUSKY WOOD-SWALLOW 7″
Artamus cyanopterus
Australia

LAFRESNAYE'S VANGA 8"
Xenopirostris xenopirostris
Madagascar

HELMET BIRD 12"
Aerocharis prevostii
Madasgacar

VANGA SHRIKES, Vangidae

Distribution: 13 species. Madagascar; in forests, brushlands, mangrove swamps. Nonmigratory.

Characteristics: 5–12". Birds with soft, rather loose plumage, typically glossy black or blue above, white below, with patches of gray or brown in some species. Bill stout, hooked, notched (thin and curved in one, casqued in another); legs and feet strong; wings rounded; tail square or rounded. Sexes alike or different.

Habits: Generally gregarious, arboreal birds; often flock with other species. Glean leaves and branches for insects, small amphibians, and reptiles. Flight strong, undulating. Breeding habits little known. Nest of one a large saucer of sticks in high tree fork; eggs of two species, white or green with brown spots.

173

LOGGERHEAD SHRIKE 7″
Lanius ludovicianus
Temperate North America

GRAY-HEADED SHRIKE 11″
Melaconotus blanchoti
East Africa

RED-BILLED HELMET SHRIKE 8″
Prionops caniceps
Madagascar

SHRIKES, Laniidae, Laniinae

Distribution: 64 species. N. America to s. Mexico, Africa, Eurasia (except Arctic), e. to Philippines, s. to New Guinea and Timor. In open woodlands, forest edges, clearings, brushlands, farmlands.

Characteristics: 6–14″. Soft-plumaged birds with proportionately large heads, stout, strong, sharply hooked and notched bills, and strong legs with sharp claws. True shrikes usually gray or brown above and white below, often with strong black or white markings on head, wings, tail. African bush shrikes bright yellows, red, greens.

Habits: Aggressive, fearless, usually solitary (helmet shrikes highly gregarious). Watch for prey from prominent perch; strike and kill with bill. Food, large insects, small vertebrates. Impale prey on thorns to tear apart and for storage. Nest bulky, deep, open cup, in trees, or shrubs. Eggs 2–6, heavily spotted on white or tinted background. Nesting patterns varied, usually largely by female.

HELMET SHRIKES, Laniidae, Prionopinae

Distribution: 9 species. Africa s. of the Sahara. In forests. Nonmigratory.

Characteristics: 7½–10″. Stiff forehead feathers project forward over nostrils. Eyes surrounded by conspicuous wattle. Black above, white or buffy below in bold patterns. Wings and tail medium to long; legs short, strong; bill stout, hooked. Sexes similar.

Habits: Gregarious, arboreal birds. Move in bands of 5–20, hunting for insects, chattering and snapping bills audibly. Cup nest of grasses in tree fork; eggs 3–4, usually pale blue, spotted brown.

174

STARLINGS, Sturnidae

Distribution: 114 species, 107 living, 4 recently extinct, 12 fossil, to Eocene of France. Eurasia s. of tree line, Africa, East Indies, n. Australia, s. Pacific Islands e. to Tuamotus. Introduced elsewhere. In all types of wooded country, agricultural lands, cities and towns. Most species migratory to some extent.

Characteristics: 6–16". Stalwart, stocky birds, with straight or slightly arched pointed bill, strong, stout legs and feet, short, squarish tail. Usually dark colored with metallic sheens; some dull gray or brown, often with white, gray, yellow, or red markings; some crested, some with facial wattles. Sexes alike and unlike; young often streaked.

Habits: Highly gregarious as a rule; may be arboreal or terrestrial. Aggressive. Walk or run on ground; fly straight and fast. Food widely varied–fruits, seeds, insects, bird eggs, small vertebrates, garbage. Garrulous, with wide range of notes, harsh calls, melodious whistles; some excellent mimics. Nest typically in tree or rock cavity; some build domed or open nests in trees or on ground. Eggs 3–7, bluish to white, immaculate or spotted. Incubation by female alone or by both sexes. Care of young by both.

BLACK-COLLARED STARLING   7"
Sturnus nigricollis
Southeast Asia

COMMON MYNA   8"
Acridotheres tristis
Southeast Asia

**SPLENDID
GLOSSY STARLING   7"**
Lamprotornis splendidus
Central Africa

175

HONEYEATERS, Meliphagidae

Distribution: 172 species, 168 living, 4 recently extinct. Australia, New Zealand, Papuan region, n. to Mariannas, e. to Samoa, Hawaii. In forests, brushlands, cultivated areas. Wide range of elevation. Some migratory.

Characteristics: 4–16". Mostly small to medium-sized; bill slender, pointed, downcurved; tongue long, protractile, brush-tipped. Wings long, pointed; tail medium to long; legs short to medium. Drab greenish-browns, grays, yellows, or bold patterns of black, white, reds. Sexes alike or unlike.

Habits: Somewhat gregarious arboreal birds, rather pugnacious. Voices loud, varied, usually musical. Feed chiefly on nectar, insects, some fruit. Nest an open cup or domed with side entrance; in branches. Eggs 2–4, white to pink with spots. Incubation by female alone or by both. Both feed young.

BLACK AND RED HONEYEATER   4½"
Myzomela rosenbergii
New Guinea

TAWNY-CROWNED HONEYEATER   6"
Meliphaga melanops
Australia

EICHHORN'S FRIARBIRD   12"
Philemon eichhorni
New Ireland, Bismarck Archipelago

**CINNAMON-BREASTED
WATTLEBIRD   9"**
Melidestes torquatus
New Guinea

SPINEBILL   6"
Acanthorhynchus superciliosus
Western Australia

177

WHITE-EYES, Zosteropidae

Distribution: 91 species, 90 living, 1 recently extinct. Africa s. of Sahara, s.w. Arabia, India to Korea, Japan, islands of Indian Ocean to Australia, New Zealand, Carolines, Samoa. In forests, brushlands, mangroves. Essentially nonmigratory.

Characteristics: 4–5½". Remarkably similar little birds, olive-green to yellowish-brown above, yellow to gray or white below, and a conspicuous white eye ring. Sexes alike. Bill slender, pointed; wings rounded, 10th primary usually absent. Tail medium, square; legs short, strong.

Habits: Gregarious, active, restless, wander in small to large flocks. Food chiefly insects, fruit, nectar. Voices weak but pleasant twittering, warbling songs. Nest an open cup in a forked branch. Eggs 2–5, unspotted white to pale blue. Both parents share all nesting duties.

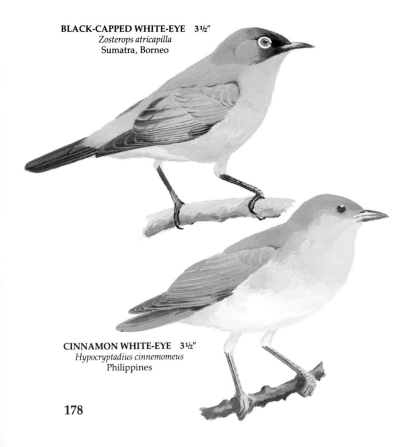

BLACK-CAPPED WHITE-EYE   3½"
Zosterops atricapilla
Sumatra, Borneo

CINNAMON WHITE-EYE   3½"
Hypocryptadius cinnemomeus
Philippines

FLOWERPECKERS, Dicaeidae

Distribution: 58 species. India to s. China, Philippines, s. to Australia, e. through Solomons. Mostly in tropical forests, scrublands; subtropical, too. Nonmigratory.

Characteristics: 3–7½". Chunky little birds with short necks, legs, tails. Bills short, stout, straight, or long, thin, curved. Wings rather long, 10th primary greatly reduced or absent. Males dark, glossy (rarely metallic) above, lighter below, with patches of red, yellow on breast, crown, or rump. Females duller.

Habits: Active inhabitants of treetops; flight rapid, darting. Feed around flowers on small insects, nectar; also tropical mistletoe berries. Sharp twittering calls. Nest a hanging pouch with side entrance. Eggs 2–3, white, rarely spotted. Nest building, incubation by female; both feed young. Diamondbirds are hole nesters; male shares duties.

ORANGE-BREASTED FLOWERPECKER 3½"
Dicaeum trigonostigma
Southeast Asia, Philippines, Malaysia

YELLOW-TAILED DIAMONDBIRD 3¼"
Pardalotus punctatus
Southeastern Australia

YELLOW-RUMPED FLOWERPECKER
Prionochilus xanthopygius
Borneo

179

SUNBIRDS, Nectariniidae

Distribution: 116 species. Africa s. of Sahara, Israel e. to c. China, Philippines, Solomons, s. through Malaya, Papuan to n. Australia. In forests, scrublands, mangroves. Most nonmigratory.

Characteristics: 3½–8½". Small birds with long, downcurved, pointed bills finely serrate near tip; tongue projectile, partly tubular, divided at tip but not brushy. Wings short, rounded; tail medium and square to long, pointed; legs short but strong. Males bright-colored in many hues, often metallic sheens; females usually much duller.

Habits: Not highly gregarious, but active arboreal birds that fly strongly; feed on nectar, insects, occasional small fruit. Voices, weak call notes, faint song. Often hover at flowers but usually perch to eat. Nest long, pendant, purse-shaped, with side entrance. Eggs 1–3, spotted or blotched on white. Incubation largely by female.

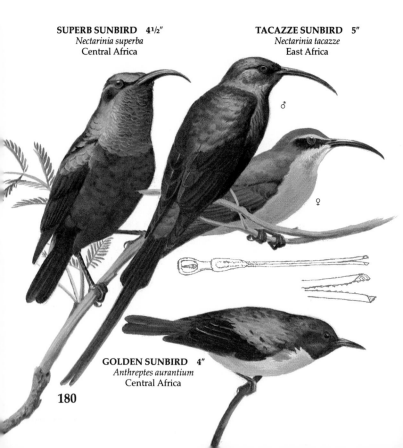

SUPERB SUNBIRD 4½"
Nectarinia superba
Central Africa

TACAZZE SUNBIRD 5"
Nectarinia tacazze
East Africa

GOLDEN SUNBIRD 4"
Anthreptes aurantium
Central Africa

BLACK-WHISKERED VIREO 6″
Vireo altiloquus
Florida and West Indies

ASHY-HEADED GREENLET 4″
Hylophilus pectoralis
Guyana, Surinam, French Guiana, Brazil, Bolivia

VIREOS, Vireonidae, Vireoninae

Distribution: 37 species. Central Canada s. to Uruguay, n. Argentina; in all types of forests, brushlands. Temperate zone species migratory.

Characteristics: 4–7″. Plain-colored small birds, olive-green to brownish gray above, yellow to gray or white below; some with light wing bars, eye rings, eye stripes; plumage never streaked or spotted, sexes alike. Bill rather heavy, slightly hooked and notched. Wings pointed or rounded, 10th primary vestigial. Legs short, strong.

Habits: Generally solitary inhabitants of forest edges and scrublands, where they search leaves and branches for insects, also eat some fruit. Movements deliberate, unhurried. Sing often; loud melodious songs of repeated phrases. Nest an open cup in branch fork, usually near ground. Eggs 2–5, white, speckled. Male helps incubate in most species; sings on nest.

181

RUFOUS-BROWED PEPPERSHRIKE 6¹/₂″
Cyclarhis gujanensis
Mexico to Argentina

CHESTNUT-SIDED SHRIKE-VIREO 7″
Vireolanius melitophrys
Mexico and Guatemala

SHRIKE-VIREOS, Vireonidae, Vireolaniinae

Distribution: 3 species. S. Mexico to central Brazil. In forests. Nonmigratory.

Characteristics: 6–7″. Loose-webbed silky plumage, greenish above, greenish-yellow to white below; head marked with stripes of yellow, black, white or gray. Bill stoutish, hooked. Sexes similar. Wings short, rounded, 10th primary reduced. Legs short, stout.

Habits: Little known and poorly studied birds of the rain forest treetops; nongregarious. Live on fruit and insects. Loud whistled song persistently repeated. Nesting unknown.

PEPPERSHRIKES, Vireonidae, Cyclarhinae

Distribution: 2 species. S. Mexico s. to Uruguay and Argentina; in open forest, brushlands. Nonmigratory.

Characteristics: 5¹/₂–7″. Loose-webbed plumage, olive-green above, greenish-yellow to buffy white below; reddish stripe above eye. Bill heavy, hooked, laterally compressed. Wings short, rounded, 10th primary reduced. Strong feet, legs. Sexes similar.

Habits: Nongregarious, found singly or in pairs; move deliberately through the foliage fairly near ground. Flight weak. Food, large insects, some fruit. Voice loud, harsh scolding, warbling song, persistently repeated. Nest a fragile cup in a branch fork. Eggs 2–3, spotted pinkish white. Natal duties by both sexes.

WOOD-WARBLERS AND WREN-THRUSH, Emberizidae, Parulinae

Distribution: 115 species. Alaska and Labrador south to Paraguay, Argentina, Peru; in forests and scrublands of all types. Northern species migratory.

Characteristics: 4–7½". Small, dainty birds with slender pointed bills, rounded tails, and pointed wings with 9 primaries. Colors varied, often bright but never glossy; grays and olive-browns dominant ground colors, variously patterned, most often with yellows, less so with reds, blues, black, white. Sexes alike and unlike.

Habits: Essentially solitary, active, arboreal (a few terrestrial) birds; feed mainly on insects; some add fruits, berries, seeds in fall and winter. One group nectar-sippers. Voices typically thin, high-pitched, weak. Migrants travel and winter in mixed flocks. Nest usually cup-shaped, in trees or shrubs; domed and on ground, or in tree cavities in a few. Eggs 2–6, white speckled with brown. Nest building, incubation by female alone; care of young by both parents.

BLACKBURNIAN WARBLER 5½"
Dendroica fusca
Eastern North America

GOLDEN-BROWED WARBLER 5"
Basileuterus belli
Mexico to Honduras

CANADA WARBLER 5"
Wilsonia canadensis
Southern Canada,
north central U.S.

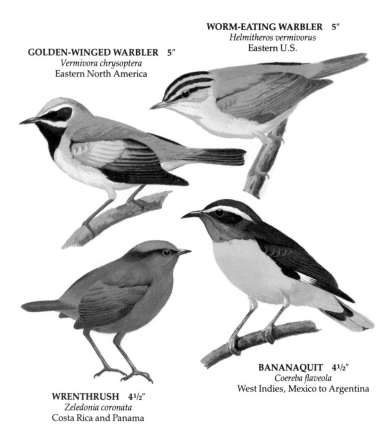

GOLDEN-WINGED WARBLER 5″
Vermivora chrysoptera
Eastern North America

WORM-EATING WARBLER 5″
Helmitheros vermivorus
Eastern U.S.

BANANAQUIT 4½″
Coereba flaveola
West Indies, Mexico to Argentina

WRENTHRUSH 4½″
Zeledonia coronata
Costa Rica and Panama

BANANAQUIT, Emberizidae, Coerebinae

Distribution: 1 species, Mexico and West Indies to Bolivia, Paraguay, n. Argentina, in woodlands, gardens, plantations. Nonmigratory.

Characteristics: 3¾–4¼″. Small bird with slender, downcurved bill, pointed wings with 9 primaries. Many subspecies. Sexes alike.

Habits: Arboreal birds, feed on nectar, insects. Voice thin, weak, high-pitched. Flit actively through foliage singly or in pairs, never in flocks. Nest an untidy ball of grass with side entrance in trees or shrubs fairly near ground. Both sexes build nest and tend young, female incubates alone.

TANAGERS, Emberizidae, Thraupinae (includes Euphonias, Conebills, Dacnises, Honeycreepers, Flower-piercers)

Distribution: 254 species. From s. Alaska and Canada south to Brazil, n. Argentina, in forests, brushlands. Temperate species migratory.

Characteristics: 3–12″. Small birds, most less than 8″; usually bright colored in bold contrasting patches of black, red, yellow, blue, brown, white. Compactly built; bill short to medium, generally notched or hooked at tip. Rictal bristles present. Wings short to long, 9-primaried; tail medium to short. Sexes alike and unlike.

Habits: Generally solitary arboreal birds that feed on fruit, berries, insects, flowers, nectar. Flight strong but not sustained. Voices not outstanding; song well developed in a few, but mainly a short warble. Nest varies from flimsy shallow cup of twigs to domed nest of grasses with side entrance; built by female, male sometimes helping. Eggs 1–5, white to greenish, usually spotted. Male may feed female on nest; always helps feed young. Incubation by female alone.

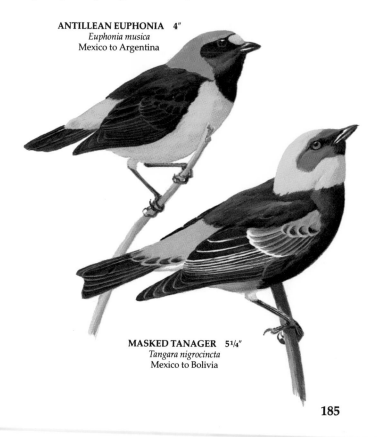

ANTILLEAN EUPHONIA   4″
Euphonia musica
Mexico to Argentina

MASKED TANAGER   5¼″
Tangara nigrocincta
Mexico to Bolivia

CARDINALS, Emberizidae, Cardinalinae (includes Saltators, Pyrrhuloxia, certain Grosbeaks and Buntings)

Distribution: 40 species. Canada south to Chile and Argentina, in forests, open country, thickets. Most northern species migratory.

Characteristics: 4½–9½″. Small birds with short, stout, conical, pointed bills; rounded wings of 9 primaries; rictal bristles usually obvious; tarsus relatively long. Colors and patterns varied, sexes unlike.

Habits: Solitary or gregarious (in nonbreeding season), arboreal or terrestrial birds that live mainly on seeds with some other vegetable matter and insects. Call notes simple chips, song varied, often well developed. Typically monogamous. Nest usually cup-shaped, in trees, shrubs, or on ground. Eggs 2–6, varied in color, marked or unmarked, incubated by female alone or both sexes. Natal care by both.

NORTHERN CARDINAL   8″
Cardinalis cardinalis
United States to s. Mexico

PYRRHULOXIA   8″
Cardinalis sinuatus
Southern U.S. to northern Mexico

SPARROWS, BUNTINGS, SEEDEATERS, Emberizidae, Emberizinae

Distribution: 315 species, 286 living, 36 fossil, to mid-Pliocene of Florida and Kansas. North and South America, Eurasia, Africa, in all types of terrestrial habitats. Most species migratory.

Characteristics: 3½–8½". Small birds with short, stout, conical, pointed bills. Gonys (see glossary) more than half length of upper bill. Rictal bristles usually obvious. Rounded wings of 9 primaries. Tarsus relatively long. Colors and patterns varied, sexes alike and unlike.

Habits: Solitary or gregarious (in nonbreeding season), arboreal or terrestrial birds, food mainly seeds, with some other vegetable matter and insects. Typically monogamous. Nest usually cup-shaped, roofed in a few tropical species, in trees, shrubs, or on ground. Eggs 2–5, incubated by female alone or by both sexes; care of young by both.

YELLOWHAMMER 6½"
Emberiza citrinella
Europe to central Siberia

REED BUNTING 6"
Emberiza schoeniclus
Eurasia

187

ORIOLES, BLACKBIRDS, GRACKLES, Emberizidae, Icterinae

Distribution: 94 species, 88 living, 29 fossil, to Pleistocene of Florida. Throughout the New World except extreme north, in almost all terrestrial habitats. Most temperate species migratory.

Characteristics: 6–21″. Small to (usually) medium-sized birds with conical, straight, pointed bills (moderately long and slender to short and stout, casqued in a few). Rictal bristles absent. Long pointed wing of 9 primaries. Tail short to long; legs and feet strong. Plumage plain or multi-colored, often solid black with metallic sheen, or bold patterns of black and yellow, orange, red, or brown. Sexes usually unlike; male larger.

Habits: Usually gregarious, sometimes highly so; either arboreal, terrestrial, or both. Eat all sorts of vegetable and animal foods. Voices generally loud, harsh, bubbling; song well developed in some. Breeding habits vary, but female usually builds nest, incubates, and feeds young; male occasionally feeds incubating female and helps irregularly in rearing young. Some build long, hanging nests; others, open cups in trees, marsh reeds, or on ground. Some nest colonially; some are polygamous; a few parasitic. Eggs 2–6, varicolored and often heavily spotted.

AUDUBON'S ORIOLE 9″
Icterus graduacauda
Texas, Mexico, Guatemala

BROWN-HEADED COWBIRD 7¹/₂″
Molothrus ater
North America

COMMON GRACKLE 12″
Quiscalus quiscula
Eastern North America

PLUSH-CAPPED FINCH, Emberizidae, Catamblyrhynchinae

Distribution: 1 species. Temperate and subtropical mountain forests of Ecuador, Colombia, Venezuela, Peru, Bolivia. Nonmigratory.

Characteristics: 6″. Bluish gray above, reddish brown below, with black on nape and sides of head, and a patch of stiff, short, orange-yellow, velvety feathers on forecrown. Bill short, thick, slightly hooked. Wings short, rounded; tail, graduated. Legs stout; feet strong. Sexes similar.

Habits: A mysterious, little-known species found sometimes in pairs or with mixed flocks of other species. Little is known of its food, breeding habits, or internal anatomy. Eats insects.

PLUSH-CAPPED FINCH   5″
Catamblyrhynchus diadema
Colombia and Venezuela to Peru, Bolivia,
and northwest Argentina

CHAFFINCH   6″
Fringilla coelebs
Europe, western Asia

CHAFFINCHES, BRAMBLING, Fringillidae, Fringillinae

Distribution: 3 species, Eurasia, Canary Islands, in open woodlands, fields, gardens. Chaffinch and brambling migratory.

Characteristics: 5½–6″. Dark gray and brown above, lighter below, with white on wings or rump. Bill conical, pointed; rictal bristles obvious; wings rounded, or 9 primaries; tail slightly forked; legs and feet strong. Sexes unlike, female duller.

Habits: Gregarious outside breeding season. Both sexes build cup-shaped nest in woods, orchards at no great height. Eggs 2–7. Incubation by female, natal care by both sexes. Calls and flight notes simple chips, songs short but melodious. Food seeds, some insects.

GOLDFINCHES AND ALLIES, Fringillidae, Carduelinae

Distribution: 112 species. Worldwide except for Australia and Pacific islands. In woodlands, scrublands. Some migratory.

Characteristics: 4–10″. Wings medium, somewhat rounded; 10th primary present, less than half length of 9th. Bill stout, conical, pointed (crossed in 2 species); gonys less than half length of upper bill. Tarsus relatively short. Color variable, some streaked and mottled, others solid patterns. Reds and yellows predominate. Sexes alike and unlike.

Habits: Gregarious birds; some nest in loose colonies. Flight strong, undulating. Song highly developed; sing in flight. Eat seeds, buds, berries, some insects. Nest, compactly woven open cup in tree branches. No nest sanitation. Eggs 3–6, usually tinted bluish and streaked and spotted. Incubation by female alone; male feeds her on nest. Care of young by both parents.

EUROPEAN GOLDFINCH   5¹/₂″
Carduelis carduelis
Europe, w. Asia, n. Africa

RED CROSSBILL   5¹/₂″
Loxia curvirostra
Circumpolar in Northern Hemisphere

COMMON REDPOLL   5¹/₂″
Carduelis flammea
N. Northern Hemisphere

HAWAIIAN HONEYCREEPERS, Fringillidae, Drepanidinae

Distribution: 28 species, 14 living, 8 species lately extinct, 10 others rare and local. Hawaiian Is.; in forests. Nonmigratory.

Characteristics: 4¹/₂–8¹/₂". Small forest birds with extremely varied bills: short, thin, pointed to long, straight to strongly curved, short, heavy hooked, but never notched or serrate. Wings pointed, 10th primary vestigial. Colors, simple grays, browns, olives, yellows, reds, or black, never glossy or metallic. Sexes unlike, or similar with male larger.

Habits: Solitary or in small loose flocks. Mostly arboreal; fairly strong fliers. Eat nectar, insects, fruit, seeds. Clear strident calls, warbling songs. Nest a simple open cup in tree, shrub, or grass clump. Eggs 2–4, white, spotted; incubated by female. Both parents feed young.

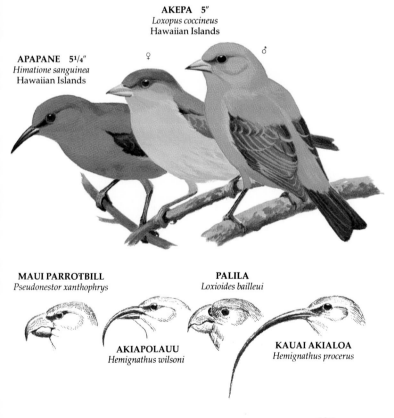

AKEPA 5"
Loxopus coccineus
Hawaiian Islands

APAPANE 5¹/₄"
Himatione sanguinea
Hawaiian Islands

MAUI PARROTBILL
Pseudonestor xanthophrys

PALILA
Loxioides bailleui

AKIAPOLAUU
Hemignathus wilsoni

KAUAI AKIALOA
Hemignathus procerus

191

TRUE SPARROWS, Passeridae (includes Snow Finches, Rock Finches)

Distribution: 29 species, 27 living, 2 fossil to middle Pleistocene. Eurasia, Africa, Malaysia, House Sparrow widely introduced throughout the world, in all types of terrestrial habitats. Nonmigratory.

Characteristics: 4–7″. Small birds with short, stout, conical, pointed bills; gonys less than half length of upper bill; rictal bristles absent. Tarsus rather short. Colors and patterns varied, most are rather drab. Sexes alike and unlike.

Habits: Somewhat gregarious, a few are loosely colonial. Primarily seed-eaters, take other vegetable matter and some insects. Voices harsh, unmelodious, no well-developed song. Nesting varied, but most build bulky, untidy nests in holes, crannies, under eaves, or in old nests of other birds. Eggs 3–6, some unmarked, others spotted or stippled. Nest building, incubation and care of young by both sexes.

♂

HOUSE SPARROW 6″
Passer domesticus
Eurasia, North Africa,
introduced widely elsewhere

im. ♂

♀

DEAD SEA SPARROW 4″
Passer moabiticus
Asia Minor

WEAVER FINCHES, Ploceidae (includes Queleas, Fodies, Bishops, Malimbas)

Distribution: 104 species. Africa, Eurasia, Madagascar, Malaysia. In fairly open country, marshes, grasslands, savannas. Nonmigratory.

Characteristics: 4–8″. Small birds, with short, stout, conical, pointed bills; gonys less than half length of upper bill. Rictal bristles absent. Tarsus relatively short. Colors and patterns widely varied. Sexes alike and unlike.

Habits: Typically gregarious; many breed colonially. Eat seeds primarily, other vegetable matter and some insects. Voices harsh, monotonous; tend to be noisy; song not well developed. Nesting highly varied. Some weave tremendous, intricate colonial nests; others make crude masses of sticks and straws; polygamy common. Eggs 2–8, usually tinted or spotted.

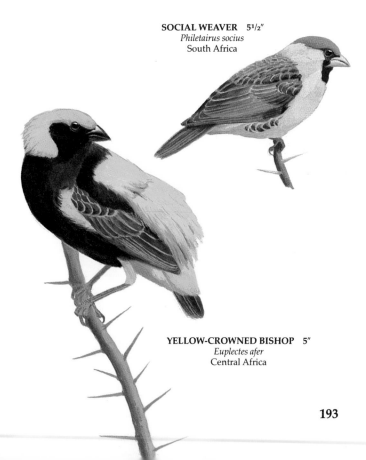

SOCIAL WEAVER   5¹/₂″
Philetairus socius
South Africa

YELLOW-CROWNED BISHOP   5″
Euplectes afer
Central Africa

WAXBILLS, Estrildidae, Estrildinae

Distribution: 107 species. Africa, southern Asia, East Indies, Australia; in open grasslands, reedy marshes, forest edges, clearings. Non-migratory.

Characteristics: 3–6″. Tiny birds of a great variety of bright colors and patterns. Bills short, stout, pointed; gonys less than half the length of upper bill. Wings short to medium, rounded to pointed; tenth primary greatly reduced. Tarsus relatively short. Sexes unlike.

Habits: Highly gregarious, lively, often in tremendous flocks; many nest colonially. Ground feeders; eat small seeds, some berries, insects. Voices weak; chirps, hisses, buzzes, chatterings; song poorly developed. Fly straight and fast for short distances. Large domed nests of various shapes, of flimsy and loose construction. Eggs 4–10, pure white. Nest building and care of young by both sexes; male usually helps with incubation.

WHITE-CROWNED MANNIKIN 4¹⁄₂″
Lonchura nevermanni
Southern New Guinea

RED-HEADED PARROT FINCH 4″
Erythura cyaneovirens
South Pacific islands

GOULDIAN FINCH 5³⁄₄″
Poephila gouldiae
Northern Australia

ORANGE-EYED PYTILIA or RED-FACED WAXBILL 4″
Pytilia afra
East Africa

PARADISE WHYDAH   15″
Vidua paradisea
Tropical Africa

**PIN-TAILED
WHYDAH   13″**
Vidua macroura
Tropical Africa

WHYDAHS, Estrildidae, Viduinae

Distribution: 9 species. Africa south of the Sahara, in open country, savannas and grasslands. Nonmigratory.

Characteristics: 3–16″. Males resplendent, glossy black above, lighter below with various other colors; tremendously long tails. Females nondescript little birds, brownish above, lighter below.

Habits: Somewhat gregarious, search for seeds and insects on the ground in small flocks. Highly parasitic and polygynous, males make display flights, circling quite high up and hovering over females. Females lay an unknown number of white eggs in nests of various waxbills.

195

MORE INFORMATION

For more details on the classification of birds and the composition of the various groups, the following titles will be helpful:

American Ornithologists' Union Committee, *Check-list of North American Birds,* 6th edition, 1983.

Austin, Oliver L., Jr., *Birds of the World,* New York, N.Y.: Golden Press, 1961.

Brodkorb, Pierce, "Catalogue of Fossil Birds," *Bulletin Florida State Museum,* 5 parts, published 1963-1978.

Bruun, Bertel, *Birds of Europe,* New York, N.Y.: Golden Press, 1971.

Gilliard, E.T., *Living Birds of the World,* New York, N.Y.: Doubleday & Co., Inc., 1958.

Peters, James L., *Check-List of Birds of the World,* Cambridge, Mass.: Harvard University Press, 13 (of 15) volumes, published 1931-1970.

Peterson, R.T., and James Fisher, *The World of Birds,* Garden City, N.Y.: Doubleday & Co., Inc., 1963.

Van Tyne, J., and A. Berger, *Fundamentals of Ornithology,* New York, N.Y.: John Wiley & Sons, Inc., 1959.

Wetmore, Alexander, *A Classification for the Birds of the World,* Washington, D.C.: Smithsonian Inst., 1960.

GLOSSARY

aftershaft a secondary feather rising from the base of the main feather.

altricial birds hatching naked and helpless and reared in the nest.

apterium (pl. apteria) a bare space between feather tracts.

booted (tarsus) undivided, unscaled (*see* scutellate).

casque a horny excrescence on the bill or head.

cere soft fleshy covering at base of upper bill.

culmen dorsal ridge of a bird's bill.

emarginate notched or slightly forked.

gape width of the mouth when opened.

gonys the ridge formed by the meeting of the two rami of the lower mandible near its tip.

gular of the throat.

lores area between the bill and eyes.

nidicolous young reared in the nest.

nidifugous young that leave the nest soon after hatching.

nucal pertaining to the nape or back of the neck.

occipital of the back of the head (occiput).

polyandry one female mating with several males.

polygamy one male mating with several females.

powder downs patches of disintegrating feathers in certain species, notably herons.

precocial precocious, young that hatch covered with down and able to move around and feed themselves.

primary one of the flight feathers attached at the hand bones (*see* secondary).

pygostyle a boney plate at the base of the tail feathers.

ramus, rami posterior sides of lower jaw that articulate with the skull.

rictal pertaining to the gape (rictus) of the mouth.

scutellate covered with scales (*see* booted).

secondary one of the flight feathers attached to the ulna (*see* primary).

syrinx the bird's "voice box."

yoke-toed with only two toes in front, two or one behind.

INDEX

As this book deals with some 400 genera involving over 2,000 popular and scientific species' names, this index has been condensed to help the reader locate the orders and families to which the commonest and most representative species belong.

199

B C D E F